P9-DSZ-155

MT SAN JACINTO COLLEGE
SAN JACINTO CAMPUS LIBRARY
1499 N STATE ST
SAN JACINTO, CA 92583

RAP AND HIP HOP

Rap and Hip Hop

EXAMINING POP CULTURE

JARED GREEN, Book Editor

Daniel Leone, President
Bonnie Szumski, Publisher
Scott Barbour, Managing Editor

GREENHAVEN
PRESS®

San Diego • Detroit • New York • San Francisco • Cleveland
New Haven, Conn. • Waterville, Maine • London • Munich

© 2003 by Greenhaven Press. Greenhaven Press is an imprint of The Gale Group, Inc.,
a division of Thomson Learning, Inc.

Greenhaven® and Thomson Learning™ are trademarks used herein under license.

For more information, contact
Greenhaven Press
27500 Drake Rd.
Farmington Hills, MI 48331-3535
Or you can visit our Internet site at http://www.gale.com

ALL RIGHTS RESERVED.
No part of this work covered by the copyright hereon may be reproduced or used in any form
or by any means—graphic, electronic, or mechanical, including photocopying, recording,
taping, Web distribution or information storage retrieval systems—without the written
permission of the publisher.

Every effort has been made to trace the owners of copyrighted material.

Cover photo: © Marko Shark/CORBIS

LIBRARY OF CONGRESS CATALOGING-IN-PUBLICATION DATA

Rap and hip hop / by Jared Green, book editor.
    p. cm.—(Examining pop culture)
Includes bibliographical references and index.
Contents: Bring the noise: the roots of rap and hip hop—Blowing up: the rise of
the hip-hop nation—Does rap glorify sex and violence?—Case study in
controversy: Eminem and gay bashing.
ISBN 0-7377-1064-0 (lib. bdg. : alk. paper) —
ISBN 0-7377-1063-2 (pbk. : alk. paper))
    1. African American youth—Social life and customs—Juvenile literature.
2. African American youth—Social conditions—Juvenile literature. 3. Rap
music—Social aspects—Juvenile literature. 4. Hip hop—Juvenile literature.
5. Popular culture—United States—Juvenile literature. 6. United States—Social
life and customs—1971- —Juvenile literature. [1. African Americans—Social life
and customs. 2. African Americans—Social conditions. 3. Rap (Music) 4. Hip hop.
5. Popular culture—History—20th century. 6. United States—Social life and
customs—1971–] I. Green, Jared. II Series.
E185.86 .R35   2003
306'.0973—dc21   2002001147

MT SAN JACINTO COLLEGE

2 1499 00000249 2

CONTENTS

while disco music was on the decline. Instead of the elite discos that primarily catered to wealthy white clients, the urban street was rap's early arena, and the music spoke both to and from a black urban experience that was rapidly taking shape as the b-boy culture of break dancing.

Chapter 2: Blowing Up: The Rise of the Hip-Hop Nation

Chapter 3: Does Rap Glorify Sex and Violence?

dards. In contrast, a critic argues that 2 Live Crew's lyrics belong to a rich African American cultural heritage and are valid and defensible free speech.

Chapter 4: Case Study in Controversy: Eminem and Gay Bashing

FOREWORD

POPULAR CULTURE IS THE COMMON SET OF ARTS, entertainments, customs, beliefs, and values shared by large segments of society. Russel B. Nye, one of the founders of the study of popular culture, wrote that "not until the appearance of mass society in the eighteenth century could popular culture, as one now uses the term, be said to exist." According to Nye, the Industrial Revolution and the rise of democracy in the eighteenth and nineteenth centuries led to increased urbanization and the emergence of a powerful middle class. In nineteenth-century Europe and North America, these trends created audiences for the popular arts that were larger, more concentrated, and more well off than at any point in history. As a result, more people shared a common culture than ever before.

The technological advancements of the twentieth century vastly accelerated the spread of popular culture. With each new advance in mass communication—motion pictures, radio, television, and the Internet—popular culture has become an increasingly pervasive aspect of everyday life.

Popular entertainment—in the form of movies, television, theater, music recordings and concerts, books, magazines, sporting events, video games, restaurants, casinos, theme parks, and other attractions—is one very recognizable aspect of popular culture. In his 1999 book *The Entertainment Economy: How Mega-Media Forces Are Transforming Our Lives*, Michael J. Wolf argues that entertainment is becoming the dominant feature of American society: "In choosing where we buy French fries, how we relate to political candidates, what airline we want to fly, what pajamas we choose for our kids, and which mall we want to buy them in, entertainment is increasingly influencing every one of those choices. . . . Multiply that by the billions of choices that, collectively, all of us make each day and you have a portrait of a society in which entertainment is one of its leading institutions."

It is partly this pervasive quality of popular culture that makes it worthy of study. James Combs, the author of *Polpop: Politics and Popular Culture in America*, explains that examining popular culture is important because it can shape people's attitudes and beliefs:

> Popular culture is so much a part of our lives that we cannot deny its developmental powers. . . . Like formal education or family rearing, popular culture is part of our "learning environment.". . . Though our pop culture education is informal—we usually do not attend to pop culture for its "educational" value—it nevertheless provides us with information and images upon which we develop our opinions and attitudes. We would not be what we are, nor would our society be quite the same, without the impact of popular culture.

Examining popular culture is also important because popular movies, music, fads, and the like often reflect popular opinions and attitudes. Christopher D. Geist and Jack Nachbar explain in *The Popular Culture Reader*, "the popular arts provide a gauge by which we can learn what Americans are thinking, their fears, fantasies, dreams, and dominant mythologies. The popular arts reflect the values of the multitude."

This two-way relationship between popular culture and society is evident in many modern discussions of popular culture. Does the glorification of guns by many rap artists, for example, merely reflect the realities of inner-city life, or does it also contribute to the problem of gun violence? Such questions also arise in discussions of the popular culture of the past. Did the Vietnam protest music of the late 1960s and early 1970s, for instance, simply reflect popular antiwar sentiments, or did it help turn public opinion against the war? Examining such questions is an important part of understanding history.

Greenhaven Press's *Examining Pop Culture* series provides students with the resources to begin exploring these questions. Each volume in the series focuses on a particular aspect of popular culture, with topics as varied as popular culture itself. Books in the series may focus on a particular genre, such as *Rap and Hip Hop*, while others may cover a specific medium, such as *Computers and the Internet*. Volumes such as *Body Piercing and Tattoos* have their focus on recent trends in popular culture, while titles like *Americans' Views About War* have a broader historical scope.

In each volume, an introductory essay provides a general

overview of the topic. The selections that follow offer a survey of critical thought about the subject. The readings in *Americans' Views About War*, for example, are arranged chronologically: Essays explore how popular films, songs, television programs, and even comic books both reflected and shaped public opinion about American wars from World War I through Vietnam. The essays in *Violence in Film and Television*, on the other hand, take a more varied approach: Some provide historical background, while others examine specific genres of violent film, such as horror, and still others discuss the current controversy surrounding the issue.

Each book in the series contains a comprehensive index to help readers quickly locate material of interest. Perhaps most importantly, each volume has an annotated bibliography to aid interested students in conducting further research on the topic. In today's culture, what is "popular" changes rapidly from year to year and even month to month. Those who study popular culture must constantly struggle to keep up. The volumes in Greenhaven's *Examining Pop Culture* series are intended to introduce readers to the major themes and issues associated with each topic, so they can begin examining for themselves what impact popular culture has on their own lives.

What Is Hip Hop?

THE ATTEMPT TO SUM UP ANY POPULAR CULTURE movement, particularly one as vital and volatile as hip hop, presents an inevitable set of problems. By the time this book is published—perhaps even by the time this introduction is written—the currently dominant artists and musical styles discussed here may already have been displaced by the unstoppable forces of hip-hop innovation. By definition, the great proportion of popular music is prone to disposability as trends both shape and follow the ever-changing tastes of the record-buying public. Even by the blink-of-an-eye pace of pop music, however, the constant drive to develop new flavors that is the engine of hip-hop success is also responsible for the notoriously short shelf-life of rap artists and their signature styles. After all, the rap industry evolves so quickly that only seven years after Dr. Dre's now-classic 1992 album *The Chronic* laid down the blueprint for the West Coast G-Funk sound, Dre's 1999 sequal, 2001, had to remind fickle audiences of the rapper's continued relevance with such songs as "Still D.R.E." and "Forgot About Dre." With such a vast, diverse, and perpetually shifting topic before us, then, the aim of this volume is not to provide a survey of rap chart-toppers but to illuminate the historical and cultural contexts that have shaped hip hop into the global phenomenon it has become.

As with all of the volumes in the Exploring Pop Culture series, this book begins with the assumption that popular culture itself is an important subject of study and that a nuanced understanding of contemporary entertainment is an essential part of cultural literacy. Of the many pop culture movements that currently influence styles, attitudes, beliefs and even politics around the world, few have had as extensive an impact as hip hop. Since its emergence as a term for the loose affiliation of African American urban street fashions (especially those associated with graffiti art and break dancing), musical forms, and vocal styles during the 1970s, hip hop has become, in author Tony Karon's words, the "most important youth culture on the planet." Def Jam cofounder and hip-hop mogul Russell Simmons goes even further, predicting that "as much as we like Shakespeare, the future's going to like DMX." Arguments over relative literary merits aside, what Simmons means is that perhaps even more so than any other popular musical form—including rock—hip hop is the musical medium through which the story of life in America at the end of the twentieth and the beginning of the twenty-first centuries is being told. Whether or not DMX himself will be studied in literature classes four hundred years from now, future scholars may well need to turn toward rap music to gain key insight into this period of American history.

Today, hip hop is in every sense a culture in its own right; it is a constellation of urban-oriented intellectual and artistic fields, including dance, art, television, film, fashion, and, of course, music, that has reached every corner of the globe. So pervasive is hip hop's influence, in fact, that it may be easy to take it for granted as a permanent feature of our cultural landscape. For anyone born after 1980—born, that is, into a world already moving to the rhythm of rap—it is nearly impossible to imagine what it might have been like to awaken one summer's day in 1979 to hear the Sugar Hill Gang's "Rapper's Delight" jumping through the radio with its urgent rhythmic hook and ricochet rhymes pinging along like a pinball machine careening toward tilt: "I said a hip, hop, the hippie, the hipidipit, hip hip, hopit, you don't stop. . . ." Would you have known that you had just heard the future of music? Now, after more than two decades have passed since the sound that would come to be recognized as rap first began to percolate throughout the boroughs of New York City, in a world forever changed by the influence of hip hop, we still might find ourselves asking what, exactly, *is* hip hop?

The short answer is that hip hop is, indeed, a culture and rap music its most visible (and audible) artistic form. As this volume will show, however, both rap and hip hop are far more complicated than this formula suggests and both have extensive histories that bear further exploration. So what is hip hop? How did it originate? Does it have a "beginning"? Can we find the seeds of hip hop by locating the very first rap song? Given how many different opinions there are on the subject, tracing the exact origin of hip hop is a bit like trying to figure out what might have been happening in the universe just moments before the big bang. Many claims have been made about what song deserves the distinction of being the first rap ever recorded: If it wasn't "Rappers Delight," then was it the Fatback Band's "King Tim III (Personality Jock)"? Was it earlier than that, in the musical poetry of the Last Poets or Gil Scott-Heron? Was it in one of James Brown's improvisational call-and-response jams or even Bob Dylan's "Subterranean Homesick Blues"? The closer we look for sources and the farther back we go, the more we have to realize that rap was not "invented" all at once but was the outgrowth of centuries of musical expression, experimentation, and innovation. As Gail Hilson Woldu reminds us, the roots of rap extend deeply into the cultural and musical history of the African diaspora. This is due, in part, to the fact that to this day rap remains principally indebted to two of America's greatest musical traditions—blues and jazz—as well as the later musical forms that they spawned, including rock, rhythm and blues, soul, and funk. Moreover, as a fundamentally African American musical form, like blues and jazz before it, rap retains traces of the folk songs and vocal and musical rhythms of Africa and the Caribbean that often served as a means of communication for African peoples forcibly transported to the United States under the yoke of slavery.

In order to grasp the multidimensionality of hip hop and fully appreciate its value in contemporary life, it is essential to regard its musical component in just such a broad historical context. This historicizing gesture requires a sort of double vision, with one lens maintaining focus on the kind of deep history Woldu demands and the other trained on the specific incarnations that have marked rap's evolution from its late–twentieth-century origins to the present day. Perhaps we might go so far as to say that hip hop springs not from any particular song so much as from the fundamentally ambivalent identity suggested by the term *African American*. It might well be argued that this ambivalence—the ability to be two things at once—is what defines the hip-hop mode and accounts for the many dazzling paradoxes of hip-hop culture.

From the dawn of the b-boy era, when DJs were just inventing the hip-hop vocabulary of scratching, cutting, and breakbeats behind the rhymes of the first MCs, to the hip-hop explosion of the late 1980s to the global industry of today, rap music has assumed many apparently contradictory guises. Consider, for example, the stress fractures that began as soon as hip-hop's potency as a subculture began to be co-opted by mainstream corporate culture. Although it was the ragged sonic collage of early rap that dragged black music out of the mostly white discos and back into the streets during the 1970s, it was a defanged, radio- and MTV-friendly and glossily pop-oriented rap—represented by acts such as MC Hammer, Vanilla Ice, and the Fresh Prince—that brought hip hop to mainstream white suburban audiences during the eighties and nineties. In spite of the political urgency of Public Enemy, the ominous narratives of Eric B. and Rakim, and the "Afrocentrism" and experimentation of Native Tongues members such as A Tribe Called Quest and De La Soul, once rap went pop, it was only a short time before advertising agencies were able to see the potential of rap music as a marketing tool to sell everything from sneakers and soda to fast food and jeans. Soon, elements of hip-hop music and aesthetics were making their presence felt on radio, television, and in the movies, but not necessarily in the form desired by those within the burgeoning hip-hop nation. As cultural critic Nelson George points out, "[While] hip hop's values are by and large fixed—its spirit of rebellion, identification with street culture, materialism, and aggression—it is also an incredibly flexible tool of communication, quite adaptable to any number of messages." This very ambivalence, according to George, accounts for why "it has been so easy to turn every element of culture associated with hip hop into a product," and the resulting commodification of the hip-hop image can be seen as compromising rap's ability to educate and empower the African American audiences to whom it was originally addressed. On the other hand, as George takes pains to stress, "hip hop survives even the crassest commercialism, or at least, it has so far." Ambivalence, then, is what allows rap music to loudly proclaim its material-ism even as its appropriation of status symbols (Hilfiger and Nautica clothing, expensive jewelry and cars, and the ubiqui-tous Cristal champagne) criticizes and undermines the racial exclusionism of a privileged class that customarily keeps a great percentage of African Americans on the margins.

The much-debated relationship between gangsta rap and the glorification of drugs and guns is also a product of the am-bivalence that makes rap seem at once a truthful witness of and a cynical contributor to a disturbing culture of inner-city vio-lence. This apparent dichotomy is surely the most vexing source of rap's perpetually problematic status in mainstream American life. As a result of its ability to speak plainly and di-rectly to young listeners, rap and hip hop have consistently at-tracted controversy from conservatives and liberals alike, yielding high-profile court cases such as the obscenity trial over 2 Live Crew's *As Nasty as They Wanna Be* and the forma-tion of the Parents Music Resource Center, which pressured the music industry to adopt the Parent's Advisory Warning sticker on albums deemed to have explicit content. Of course, hip hop has always thrived on its ability to challenge the mu-sical, political, and cultural status quo, and although it may seem almost quaint to readers today to imagine that the Adidas-and-gold-medallion-clad rappers of the early 1980s were once looked upon as figures of menace, Juan Williams's article "Fighting Words: Racism, Sexism, and Homophobia in Pop and Rap," first published in 1989, reminds us that con-cerns about the negative social impact of degrading, porno-graphic, and violent lyrical content (in rock music as well as hip hop) have been in the public consciousness for quite some time. The aura of danger that has surrounded much of hip hop from the beginning is due not to the content of any particular artist's work, but rather is traceable to attitudes about rap mu-sic's link to the so-called underclass (a predominantly black and Hispanic population concentrated in some of America's most economically depressed urban centers). As rap evolved beyond simple boasts and party rhymes and developed an in-creasingly political consciousness with the emergence of such groups as Public Enemy and Boogie Down Productions (BDP), the music's role as an observer of and commentator on the social realities of the underclass came to the foreground. Whereas Public Enemy and BDP sought to raise the awareness of young African Americans with such anthems as "Fight the Power" and "Self Destruction," respectively, others avoided high-minded rhetoric in favor of angry provocation, as exemplified by NWA [Niggaz wit' Attitude]'s 1988 diatribe, "F——k Tha Police."

As Robin D.G. Kelley suggests, perhaps no aspect of hip hop has garnered—or profited from—controversy quite like gangsta rap. As gangsta rap developed from its earliest articulations, such as BDP's *Criminal Minded* to Ice-T's and NWA's unvarnished stories of desperation, crime, and police brutality in Los Angeles's infamous South Central region, and finally into a popular genre that cashed in on the player glamour of guns, money, drugs, and sex, a blurring of the lines between rap's facts and its fantasies, between the characters rappers play and the lives they lead, became inevitable. The debate over rap music's influence shows no sign of diminishing, and the basic

19

questions remain—as they were back when Juan Williams was writing—essentially as follows: Do expressions of violence or depictions of drug use and sexual promiscuity in rap lyrics encourage these same behaviors, do they simply report on unpleasant and customarily underrepresented realities, or both?

On the one hand, many hip-hop artists have long used rap music as a way to represent the trials and privations of inner-city life that they have experienced or witnessed. Public Enemy's Chuck D. famously dubbed rap music "black America's CNN," and indeed it has served as a potent tool for reporting on injustices and hardships that often escape mainstream attention. On the other hand, the line that divides truthful representation from exploitation is not always entirely clear, and although some artists rap about black-on-black gang violence, drug abuse, and the desperation that leads to crime in order to critique such conditions, others use the same material to spin fantasies about the dark glamour of criminal life. When "keeping it real" gets inextricably linked with "being hard," and become synonymous with both carrying weapons, committing crimes, or serving time in prison, it can often be difficult to distinguish between reality and representation. Such confusion has had deadly consequences for rap's fans and its stars alike, as was made most tragically evident by the 1996 and 1997 slayings of Tupac Shakur and the Notorious BIG, two of gangsta rap's brightest lights. While Tupac's and Biggie's deaths threw the lethal consequences of "thug life" into stark relief, according to Ronin Ro, the true threat has always been to the young consumers under the spell of the gangsta's promised lifestyle:

> While the mainstream media haggled over censorship issues surrounding the music, the gangsta rappers began translating their on-wax fantasies into full-scale reality. Many were soon entangled in legal problems and shootouts, and their listeners grew further entranced. Soon, the listener—young, lacking role models or authority figures, and somewhat bored with life—would accept the gangsta rapper's lyrics as gospel.

The often invisible irony is that even rappers with gang backgrounds or actual criminal records hire image consultants to ensure that the dangerous veneer required to maintain gangsta success is kept up to date.

In spite of its prominence in the media, rap-related violence is not the only point of contention when it comes to lyrical content. As focused as the music may be on addressing racial inequalities, misogyny and homophobia are still widely accepted, and women and gays continue to be singled out as the targets of some of rap's most vicious attitudes. The problem has not just been limited to lyrics, either; gender-based inequality has had consequences for female artists trying to make names for themselves in hip hop, and although there have been women in the industry from the start, they have had to struggle for equal visibility and air time. Thankfully, a great deal has changed with the success of contemporary female rap stars and entrepreneurs such as Queen Latifah, Lauryn Hill, Lil' Kim, Eve, and Missy Elliott; however, they remain vastly outnumbered by men, and it is still common to hear gangsta rap depictions of women as little more than money-mad nuisances or expendable sex objects. Similarly, in the male-dominated rap industry, the privileging of a particular vision of heterosexual masculinity has left little—if any—room for homosexual identity. Although the examples of highly successful female vocal groups and solo artists are easily identifiable, one would have to look deeply into hip hop's obscure underground to find any rap acts who are openly gay. Far more typical are lyrics that reserve little else beside disdain for homosexuality and that, at their worst, appear to condone intolerance and even outright violent attitudes toward gays. As music critic Chris Noris pointedly laments, "Being a hip-hop head has always meant having to say you're sorry—to Jews for liking Public Enemy; to the police for liking N.W.A.; to Koreans for liking Ice Cube; to women for liking just about anybody."

This last aspect of hip hop's fundamental ambivalence shows no sign of diminishing. One need only cast a glance at the recent trajectory of Eminem, the Detroit rapper who is currently one of the most successful—and most hotly debated—rap acts in the world. After the release of *The Marshall Mathers LP* in 2000, it seemed that no one was without a strong opinion about Eminem and his alter ego, Slim Shady, who has been the mouthpiece for some of the darkest and most explicit fantasies of sex and violence ever recorded in rap music. Well into 2001, virtually everywhere one looked, somebody was talking about Eminem, praising his lyrics, his black humor, his flow on the mic, or condemning his misogyny and homophobia as a toxin in the bloodstream of America.

No matter where one stands on the Eminem debate, it is important to keep in mind that controversy over music's influence on young listeners neither begins nor ends with *The Marshall Mathers LP*. For that matter, it is not even a special quality of rap music to offer itself as the voice of rage and rebellion: The ability to provoke mainstream outrage is an inherent and even necessary aspect of what makes many popular musical forms vital and appealing to their audiences.

Reporter, entertainer, provocateur, educator, tastemaker, corrupter—what, in the end, is hip hop? With as many different perspectives on the topic as there are vocal styles and subgenres to the music, ultimately there can be no satisfying answer to gather this culture's complexities under one single definition. Poet and author Greg Tate's often-reprinted (and even recorded, sampled, and remixed) poem, "What Is Hip Hop?" obtains its power by tapping into the always and inexhaustibly dual nature of hip hop:

> hip hop is not what it is today but what it could be
>   tomorrow
> hip hop is pumas and a hoodie today but why not leather
>   fringe and sequins mañana?
> If hip hop wanted to be that corny who could argue with it
>   but a nigga who was faded?
> Arguing with hip hop about the nature of hip hop is like
>   arguing with water about the nature of wetness
> Like Bunny Wailer said
> some tings come to ya and some tings come at ya but hip
>   hop flows right through ya . . .
> hip hop is what happened when the black community lost
>   track of itself on the radar screen of Reaganomics
> the blip that boombipped turned up to announce black is
>   back all in we're gonna exterminate our own next of kin.
> hip hop is beyond black nationalism
> hip hop is not hung up on countersupremacy
> it reigns supreme like all dope fiends
> hip hop is half black and half japanese
> digital chips on the shoulders of african lips

hip hop is black prozac
hip hop is black sadomasochism
where the hurting ends and the feeling begins.

Looking back over the last quarter of the twentieth century, perhaps Chuck D. put it best when he said, "Hip hop is just black people's creativity, and we've always been creative people. So it's just a term for the last twenty-five years." Looking forward toward the shape of things to come, Mos Def's "Fear Not of Man" is even more expansive in its vision of hip hop as nothing less than the beating heart of the world: "People be askin' me all the time/ What's gonna happen with hip hop?/ I tell them, you know what's gonna happen with hip hop?/ Whatever's happening with us."

EXAMINING POP CULTURE

Bring the Noise: The Roots of Rap and Hip Hop

Contextualizing Rap: A Brief History of African American Music

Gail Hilson Woldu

Although modern hip-hop culture and rap music as we know it emerged in New York City during the mid to late 1970s, both have their roots in the long history of the African diaspora. The music that served as a common language between disparate African peoples who had been separated from their lands, language groups, and cultures by the American slave trade led to diverse forms of African American music, including gospel, blues, and jazz. Contemporary rap is the offspring of a combination of musical and performance styles from blues and jazz (and, in turn, rock, soul, and funk), and hip-hop culture continues to be informed by the folkloric figures that suffuse these traditions. Gail Hilson Woldu is an assistant professor of music at Trinity College in Hartford, Connecticut.

[OUR UNDERSTANDING OF MODERN RAP AND hip hop] ought to depend on a clear understanding of rap's musical and literary antecedents. If, for example, we are to embrace [critic] Houston Baker's contention that rap is classical black sound, we must consider rap's expressive forebears and determine how firmly rap is grounded in these traditions. In

■

Excerpted from "Contextualizing Rap," by Gail Hilson Woldu, *New Approaches to the Twentieth Century: American Popular Music*, edited by Rachel Rubin and Jeffrey Melnick (Amherst: University of Massachusetts Press, 2001). Copyright © 2001 by Gail Hilson Woldu. Reprinted with permission.

understanding the continuum of black musical expressions, we can better understand the corollaries between rap and other black music. We must explore the influence of traditions of black expression on rap, from the African griot [a musical storyteller] through the [African American folkloric figure] Signifying Monkey, the fabled trickster Shine and mythical badman Stagolee, the blueswomen of the 1920s, and the Last Poets. We need to understand these expressive relationships in order to fully appreciate the importance of [critic] Kephra Burns's observation that black people "were rapping in the 1850s: trading tall tales, handing out verbal abuse in rhymes, and providing [their] own rhythmic, chest-whacking, thigh-slapping accompaniment." In particular, we must consider the language and the roles of rap—especially its extramusical functions as cultural actor and critic. Indeed, if we are to accept [rapper] Luther Campbell's contention that 2 Live Crew's texts are "nothing but a group of fellas bragging," we need, as [Professor] Henry Louis Gates has suggested (see "2 Live Crew, Decoded," page 101), to become "literate in the vernacular traditions of African Americans" and understand the group's "exuberant use of hyperbole (phantasmagoric sexual organs, e.g.)" in terms of "black cultural codes." And if we seek to challenge allegations that rap is not music, we must go further still. We need to explore music-making practices of the African diaspora, in particular those of the Caribbean (what counts as music outside Western culture does not always comport with European definitions) and understand how rap borrows from these different norms. At every turn, we must develop a historical context.

Slave Protest Music

A convenient starting point for this discussion is the "protest" music of the slaves and, more generally, the nature of music making among the slaves. In his study of black culture, Lawrence Levine writes that song in African cultures "served the dual purpose of not only preserving communal values and solidarity but also providing occasions for the individual to transcend, at least symbolically, the inevitable restrictions of his environment and his society by permitting him to express deeply held feelings which ordinarily could not be verbalized."

Similarly in early African American slave communities the centrality of song and other expressive arts including tales, proverbs, jokes, and aphorisms reflected the importance accorded verbal improvisation and the significance of the spoken arts for "uphold[ing] traditional values and group cohesion." Through song, slaves were also able to voice criticism. In slave protest music we find examples of early diasporic antecedents for the style and messages of rap. The amount of this nineteenth-century rebellious music that survives pales in comparison with that of other slave musics, but there is a sig-

Black Women on the Margins

Black woman rappers interpret and articulate the fears, pleasures, and promises of young black women whose voices have been relegated to the margins of public discourse. They are integral and resistant voices in rap music and in popular music in general who sustain an ongoing dialogue with their audiences and with male rappers about sexual promiscuity, emotional commitment, infidelity, the drug trade, racial politics, and black cultural history. By paying close attention to female rappers, we can gain some insight into how young African-American women provide for themselves a relatively safe free-play zone where they creatively address questions of sexual power, the reality of truncated economic opportunity, and the pain of racism and sexism. Like their male counterparts, they are predominantly resistant voices that at times voice ideas that are in sync with elements of dominant discourses. Where they differ from male rappers, however, is in their thematic focus. Although male rappers' social criticism often contests police harassment and other means by which black men are "policed," black women rappers' central contestation is in the arena of sexual politics.

Tricia Rose, *Black Noise.* University Press of New England, 1994.

nificant enough body to make it worth considering. The images in "Many Thousand Go" make a powerful statement
against the cruelties of slavery, and the repeated words "no
more" suggest, at the very least, the possibility of retribution:

> No more peck o' corn for me, No more, no more;
> No more peck o' corn for me, Many thousand go.
> No more driver's lash for me.
> No more pint o' salt for me.
> No more hundred lash for me.
> No more mistress' call for me.

. . . More common are songs that "sing the master." In
these, slaves commented on—and often lampooned—their
masters' behavior and habits. The language was typically jocular, with texts that might call attention to the master's attire,
courting habits, or treatment of his slaves. The texts could also
be condemnatory, however, and encoded in such a way as to be
understood only by the slaves themselves—and misunderstood
by the targets. This tradition of "employing song or rhyme for
making oral commentary" derives from bardic forms common
in areas of west and central Africa. Rife with parody, exaggeration, and satire, the songs relied on slaves' improvisatory skills
to entertain their fellows, usually at their masters' expense.
Like their modern-day Caribbean confreres, slave "toasters,"
or "plantation men-of-words,". . . won the esteem of both their
peers and masters by rhyming and improvising well:

> The ability to improvise, to make rhymes and to lead while
> entertaining, was highly valued by planter and slave alike.
> The good rhymer might use his wits to confront others in
> situations which otherwise would have resulted in whipping.
> . . . Slaves could gain some advantage in encounters with
> their masters by drawing on their abilities to improvise wit-
> tily. And in such situations, they often used irony to launch
> moral commentary at certain figures who made claims for
> themselves as agents of benevolence.

"Signifying," a term often described as an allusive way of
"talking bad," was a vital component of singing the master. The
roots of this verbal play are in the practices of griots, West
African professional singers who "combine the functions of liv-

ing history book and newspaper with vocal and instrumental virtuosity." Exaggeration reigned supreme and outright lies were not uncommon. In discussing the oft-cited slave song "Roun' de Corn, Sally," planter James Hungerford recalled that the music "caused much amusement at the expense of each one of us who in turn became the subject of satire." Truths were stretched in this song, and words were added on the spot. . . .

"Playing the Dozens"

Decades later, signifying, also known as "playing the dozens" (or simply "the dozens") would figure prominently in the verbal contests omnipresent in African American culture. These improvised wars of wits are central to African American entertainment—featured in the black vaudeville shows of the early 1900s, the comedy routines of Redd Foxx and Moms Mabley, the poetic mouthing-off of the young Muhammad Ali, and the verbal shootouts of MCs in the Bronx—and are a mainstay of the boasting, toasting, and bragging found in much rap. There was, of course, no immediate jump from slave music, with its good-humored mocking and tongue-in-cheek teasing, to rap's ad hominem attacks. The path to rap and its numerous styles lies in the spectrum of popular Afrodiasporic musics from the postbellum years to the 1970s. Roxanne Shanté's "revenge" raps, in which she names and belittles the sexual prowess of her male competitors; KRS-ONE's derision of C. DeLores Tucker [chair of the National Political Congress of Black Women]; and Public Enemy's attacks on virtually everyone including Elvis Presley and John Wayne are all rooted in the traditions of the savannah griots and African American slaves, and are part of a musical history that grew from the practices of the blueswomen of the 1920s, the rhythm-and-blues singers of the 1950s and 1960s, and the protest culture of the 1960s and 1970s.

Parallels abound in the music of black blueswomen of the 1920s and 1930s and female rappers of the 1980s and 1990s. Social issues documented in the music of blueswomen Ma Rainey, Ida Cox, and Bessie Smith are strikingly similar to those of rappers Queen Latifah, Lil' Kim, and the Lady of Rage, as are the women's manners of performance. The issues that predominate in both genres center largely on women's relationships with men and in some instances respond directly to men's opinions about women. . . .

Black Women Find a Voice

If the music of the blueswomen was a valorization of black women's experiences in the 1920s and 1930s, intended to ennoble and make heroes of ordinary black women, that of Queen Latifah, Salt-n-Pepa, the Lady of Rage, Lil' Kim, and Lauryn Hill is a checklist of black women's complaints in the 1980s and 1990s. Though the music of black female rappers resonates most clearly among young black women, the themes often center on a broad spectrum of women's issues. In this sense, the music is a late twentieth-century corollary to that of the classic blues singers: it is by turns catholic in appeal, with themes that can be embraced by young women of various races and ethnicities, and intended to inspire black women in particular. Its audiences, though, like those of the blueswomen, are both male and female; as a consequence, [writes cultural critic Tricia Rose,] "black women rappers are in dialogue with one another, with male rappers, with other popular musicians (through sampling and other revisionary practices), with black women fans, and with hip hop fans in general."

According to Tricia Rose, black women rappers "interpret and articulate the fears, pleasures, and promises of young black women whose voices have been relegated to the margins of public discourse." She points to three predominant themes—"heterosexual courtship, the importance of the female voice, and mastery in women's rap and black female public displays of physical and sexual freedom"—and argues against those assessments of women's rap that limit discussion to two areas: 1) that "women rappers are feminist voices who combat sexism in rap"; and 2) that "the sexist exclusion or mischaracterization of women's participation in rap music devalues women's significance and must be countered by evidence of women's contributions." Angela Davis takes Rose's arguments a step further, offering a broader perspective on black women's music. She says that the music must be considered in the context of the collective consciousness of the black community, influenced by and influencing black social and political identities ("Black Women"). In this sense, then, black women's popular music becomes inextricably linked to any understanding of black culture and central to the documentation of black American cultural development.

Song and Self Empowerment

The music of Queen Latifah and Salt-n-Pepa defines a generation. With such titles as "None of Your Business," "Negro Wit' an Ego," "Let's Talk about Sex" and "Ladies First," their music is an organ for the complex intersection of race and gender in late twentieth-century black American popular culture. These women belong to the first generation of female rappers whose influence was at its peak in the early 1990s. Latifah, in particular, came to epitomize the black woman's voice in a male-dominated industry. Her name reminds us of the many blues "queens" some sixty years earlier and hints at a female-centered musical monarchy. Latifah has a reputation as a role model that rests as much on her demeanor as on the themes in her music. Her hard-edged, in-your-face style made possible her entrance into a domain that did not want her. In this regard Latifah differs from the blueswomen, who set the standards for and defined a tradition in music rather than infiltrated it. Latifah's landmark "Ladies First" addresses this dilemma, announcing with no apologies and much bravado a statement about her qualifications to rap that Ma Rainey and her generation would have found quite unnecessary.

Latifah's swagger reaches new levels in the music of the Lady of Rage. Rage's street-tough style of bragging—absent in the music of the blueswomen—is akin to that of KRS-ONE and grounded in the most aggressive tradition of playing the dozens. Sex as a theme is noticeably absent in this music; what matters here is a toe-to-toe, flow-for-flow battle of words. In fact, Rage consciously avoids raps with provocatively sexy rhymes because she wants parents to feel comfortable letting their children listen to her music. It is little surprise that Rage's first CD, *Necessary Roughness*, was produced by Suge Knight on the Death Row [recording] label; Rage's style is similar to that of other Death Row artists, whose roster has included Tupac Shakur, Dr. Dre, and Snoop Doggy Dogg—aggressive and angry. The title cut tells us as much about Rage's style as it does about how she perceives herself in the male-centered rap industry:

I strikes hard like Ben Frank's lightnin' rod,
Leave you suckas scarred, leave U suckas charred.
Now you're burnt to a crisp, so check the vocalist . . .
Then I shoot from the jugular, I get ruff and ruggeder
You can't front on this big bodied southerner . . .

Sex as a theme is as dominant in the music of black female rappers as it was in the music of the blues queens. Like the blueswomen, black female rappers challenge our notions of sexuality and femininity. They flaunt their bodies, demand parity in sexual relationships, and prove, through their lyrics and personal affairs, that they can be as sexually aggressive as men. Rappers Salt-n-Pepa are known for the carefully crafted insouciance of their stage presence as they shake their behinds suggestively, rapping "my jeans fit nice, they show off my butt," while Foxy Brown and Lil' Kim are infamous for the raps that mention specific sex acts. The messages are often confounding and contradictory because, as Rose writes, just as women rappers affirm their own physical beauty in raps that call attention to the sensuality of black women's bodies, they simultaneously perpetuate and permit objectification of the black female body. This doubleness has been explained in two important ways: (1) as self-inflicted exploitation; and (2) as a rejection of white American standards of physical beauty. . . .

The Legacy of the 1960s

Rap's intense focus on sexual politics is just one obvious manifestation of the deep debt that it owes to earlier forms of African American music. The most direct ancestors of rap were the various African American artists making political music in the 1960s. From the Freedom Singers to James Brown, the musicians of the 1960s wrote music that responded to the unsettled times and gave rise to the styles and messages now prevalent in rap. As the musical spokespersons for the Civil Rights movement, the Freedom Singers toured the United States spreading the words of Martin Luther King Jr. and particularly the Student Nonviolent Coordinating Committee. Their close harmonies, almost always sung a cappella, reflected a congregational song style and a church heritage that presupposed audience interaction. Martin Luther King Jr. wrote that these freedom songs were "more than just incantations of clever phrases designed to invigorate a campaign." Bernice Johnson Reagon, one of the original Freedom Singers, considered the songs her own, to be used whenever and for whatever she needed: "There is a way in which those songs kept us from being touched by people who would want us not to be who we were becoming." More important, according to Reagon the songs were "more powerful than conversation. They became a major way of making people who were not on the scene feel the intensity of what was happening in the South.". . .

In the wake of the Civil Rights movement there were increasingly militant approaches to black equality in music that responded to the new, more aggressive, and pointedly Afrocentric messages. Some of the music reflected the ideology of Malcolm X and the Black Panthers; other music looked to Africa for cultural relevance. Nowhere are African bardic traditions better realized than in the music of the Last Poets. From their first album, *The Last Poets* (1972), to *Time Has Come* (1997), the Last Poets have embodied the spirit of the griot. Their early music is modeled after West African practices, with its minimalist drumming and half-spoken, half-sung vocal delivery intended to accentuate the importance of the words, which are meant to inform, provoke, anger, and incite. Rooted in the protests of the 1960s, this music embraced the messages of the period's social activists, particularly those who advocated self-determination and self-sufficiency. The messages of the group were aimed at black people, and the harsh texts were intended to be a clarion call to those mired in complacency. . . .

Rap as Storytelling

Given their uncompromising style, it is not surprising that the Last Poets inspired younger musicians. The messages espoused and traditions embraced by this maverick pre-rap group have been adopted by a host of new rappers and adapted to the issues of the 1980s and 1990s. Many younger rappers are drawn especially to the teaching aspect of the Last Poets. From KRS-ONE to Ice-T, Ice Cube, Tupac, and Biggie Smalls, rappers have infused their music with similarly bold social and political statements meant to be heard and heeded.

Much of this music sermonizes, rounding out its raps-cum-stories with a moral. In "Once upon a Time in the Projects," Ice Cube spins a disturbing yarn about the consequences of dating the wrong girl. Replete with references to teenage pregnancy, drugs, child neglect, police harassment, and incarceration, this twisted urban fairy tale attributes the hapless storyteller's fate to his involvement, and concludes with a one-line moral: "Don't mess with a projects girl." Biggie Smalls, a.k.a. the Notorious B.I.G., takes a critical look at contemporary lifestyles and compares them with those gone by in his nostalgic "Things Done Changed." The picture he paints of life "back in the day" as being simple and family-centered contrasts sharply with his portrait of life in the 1990s. The juxtaposition of images from the past and present reminds us of our failings and tacitly implores us to do better:

> Back in the day our parents used to take care of us,
> Look at them now; they're even fuckin' scared of us.
> Calling the city for help because they can't maintain,
> Damn, shit done changed . . .
> Damn, what happened to the summertime cookout?
> Everytime I turn around a nigger getting took out.

Though it would be at once naive and incorrect to contend that storytelling and sermonizing are the sole provenance of African American literary and musical culture, it is neither to state that they are defining characteristics of African American literary and musical traditions. The incorporation of these aspects in the music of Ice Cube and Biggie Smalls, whether intentional or coincidental, extends the continuum and grounds it in practices that antedate the 1990s. . . .

The traditions of the African griots that were embraced in the work of the Last Poets are the cornerstone of KRS-ONE's music. In fact, in heralding himself as the master of "edutainment," KRS-ONE intentionally assumes the role of the griot and embraces its traditions. In "MCs Act Like They Don't Know," he raps, "Now we got white kids calling themselves niggers. The tables turn as the crosses burn. Remember you must learn"; the rapper is spreading the word, in his role as village bard, that we must learn about the past in order to understand the ironies of the present. For KRS-ONE, to be an

MC is to be a griot, interpreting current events and infusing raps with historically based and culturally relevant rhymes. Though not all would agree with his audacious revisions of Western history and his allegations that "history, no matter how you look at it, is a lie," "the teacher," as KRS-ONE is sometimes called, has established a reputation for encouraging his listeners to read and learn. Many of his raps ask black people to understand the historical basis for their status in this country. Virtually all boast of his omniscience. In his multi-themed "Edutainment," KRS-ONE says that he is more concerned with stopping fear and ignorance than climbing the charts, warns us of Christianity's duplicitous history, and tells us to always "be guided by edutainment."

Lauryn Hill's unique style of storytelling combines a panoply of Afrodiasporic musical styles: reggae, rhythm and blues, soul, and gospel. The highest-profile member of the Fugees, Hill is part of a new wave of rappers whose music is "re-pairing hip hop's weak gangsta lean" with the integrity of its messages and reaching an audience of "thug niggas, grand-mothers, and surfer dudes alike." Her music transcends hip-hop's trends, yet embodies all that hip-hop is. In "Forgive Them Father," Hill tells her listeners, with lilting, Caribbean-accented raps and singing that mixes soul and gospel styles, to beware of false friends in sheep's clothing. With its references to Cain and Abel, Caesar and Brutus, and Jesus and Judas, this song is Hill's statement about duplicitous black "brothas and sistas" who value fame and fortune more than friendship and virtue. "Doo Wop (That Thing)" is a strong message to black men and women about black pride, responsibility, and self-respect.

Frank Williams's article in *The Source* on the Lady of Rage concludes with a list of criteria for rap: "battling, storytelling, poetry, soul searching and pulling yourself out of the ghetto." Interestingly, but not surprisingly, these are also components of much music of the African diaspora, including jazz, soul, R & B, reggae, and certainly blues. If we acknowledge these as defining elements—classic characteristics . . .—of black music, rap finds its historical contexts in black art forms that can be traced to Africa and that were cultivated in the United States for over three hundred years.

In the Beginning: The Early Days Remembered

S.H. Fernando Jr.

S.H. Fernando Jr. is a Brooklyn-based music producer and the author of *Exploring the Music: Culture and Attitudes of Hip Hop*. He has contributed articles to the *New York Times, Rolling Stone, VIBE,* and *Source*. Here, Fernando fondly recalls the summer of his eleventh year, when the pathbreaking artists of rap and hip hop first exploded in clubs, at block parties on city streets, and on urban radio stations.

IN THE SUMMER OF '79, I WAS JUST ANOTHER 11-year-old on an endless quest for fun. Between watching reruns of *Speed Racer* and *The Munsters*, playing ball, and riding my bike, life was idyllic. These were indeed the "Good Times" immortalized by Chic in their hit that was all over the radio those sunny months.

But that fall, an even more memorable hit came from a group that nobody had ever heard of before. The Sugarhill Gang, as they were known, borrowed Chic's consummately funky rhythm, but instead of singing over it, they spewed an endless stream of rhymes—"I said a hip, hop, the hippie, the hipidipit, hip, hip, hopit, you don't stop." This catchy tune, called "Rapper's Delight," went on to sell over two million copies worldwide, peaking at No. 4 on the *Billboard* R&B charts and No. 36 on the pop charts on its way to becoming a Top 10 hit across the planet. It was the world's introduction to

■

Excerpted from "Back in the Day: 1975–1978," by S.H. Fernando Jr., *The VIBE History of Hip Hop*, edited by Alan Light (New York: Three Rivers Press, 1999). Copyright © 1999 by VIBE Ventures. Reprinted with permission.

hip hop, even though a lesser-known rap song by Brooklyn's Fatback Band called "King Tim III (Personality Jock)" actually came out a few months earlier on Spring Records.

Little did we know back then that this "fad" called rap was breaking out of the underground on its way to becoming a multimillion-dollar industry, as well as one of the most influential and popular musical phenomena of this century. But as much as we owe to the Sugarhill Gang and "Rapper's Delight," there is a whole history and culture that laid the groundwork for that success. Rap wasn't built in a day. It connects to an oral tradition that spans a legacy from radio jocks to doo-wop, Bo Diddley to bebop, prison toasts and idle boasts, all the way back to the African griots. More specifically, however, the birth of rap as we know it can be directly traced back to the concrete jungles of the Bronx in the late '60s and early '70s, an era now fondly remembered as the old school.

Before the term "hip hop" ever came into vogue to describe this movement, there were outdoor parties in public parks at which a DJ would patch his sound system directly into a streetlight's power box and play records as people gathered around to dance, rhyme over the beats, or write graffiti. "It was a form of recreation," recalls Richie "Crazy Legs" Colon, who went on to become a member of the legendary Rock Steady breakdancing crew. "A lot of these people didn't really have the money to join a community center around the way as far as baseball, softball, boxing, or things like that."

The Early DJ Scene

No man deserves more credit for planting the seeds of hip hop than Clive Campbell (a.k.a. Kool Herc). . . .

Popular club DJs like Pete "DJ" Jones kept the Manhattan crowds moving to a nonstop mix of trendy disco hits, cleverly blended from one song to the next; in Brooklyn, DJs Flowers and Maboya pulled the crowds, and Disco King Mario held it down in the Bronx. While these DJs did the same old thing with the newest records, Herc was creating something completely new out of old and obscure records. He noticed that funk, the era's quintessential black sound, elicited a much greater crowd reaction in the predominantly black and Hispanic Bronx. Not only that, but Herc noticed that when he played, for example, James Brown's "Give It Up or Turnit A Loose," people went especially wild during the "break" segment of the song, when just the drums or percussion took over.

Herc wondered what would happen if he got two copies of the same record and cut back and forth between them in order to prolong the break or sonic climax. Unwittingly, Herc had stumbled upon the breakbeat, the starting point for much hip hop, dance, techno, and jungle (drum 'n' bass) today. His serious devotees, the dancers who saved their best moves for the break segment, became known as break boys, or simply b-boys. . . .

As Herc ruled the Bronx during the early '70s—playing at places that now exist only as memories, like the Twilight Zone, Hevalo, and the Executive Playhouse—his style became legendary among the area's underprivileged youth. Though most kids couldn't get past the velvet ropes at pricey Manhattan clubs to see DJs like Hollywood and Eddie Cheeba, they would brave their parents' wrath to stay out late and hear [Herc's sound system] the Herculords jam in the park with MCs (Masters of Ceremony or "mike controllers") like Coke La Rock, Luvbug Starski, and Busy Bee inciting the crowds to have a good time and the original b-boys, the Nigga Twins, showing them how. One such impressionable youth was Afrika Bambaataa, a student at Adlai Stevenson High School and a resident of the Bronx River Projects in the borough's notorious south side.

A Movement Grows in New York

The South Bronx was tough turf, characterized by burned-out buildings, brutal street gangs, and the scourge of drugs and poverty, and Bambaataa was hardly a saint. As a leader of the city's biggest and baddest street gang, the Black Spades, he commanded the respect of his peers with intelligence, a sharp tongue, and a bold vision of what his black and Hispanic brothers and sisters could accomplish if they worked toward a common cause. Even as a Spade, he held the drug dealers in his area at bay and formed the Organization, uniting several different projects against the threat of violence and drugs. This initial community activism proved to be the blueprint for Bam's Zulu Nation, today known as the Universal Zulu Nation, an international hip hop movement that upholds such principles as knowledge, wisdom, understanding, freedom, justice, equality, peace, unity, love, and respect in their manifesto. Back in the day, though, the Zulus, who provided security at Bam's parties, were all about breakdancing, writing graffiti, and furthering the emerging culture of the streets known as hip hop. . . .

By 1975, as the street gangs were literally imploding due to violence, drugs, and police crackdowns, Bam's attention turned increasingly to throwing parties—first at his own projects, then at high schools and PAL (Police Athletic Leagues) parties, before taking his troupe of DJs, breakdancers, MCs, and graffiti artists all over the Tri-State Area under the banner of the Zulu Nation (in 1981, the Zulus would also be the first hip hop ambassadors to bring the beat to Europe). In this era before rap records, recalls Jazzy Jay, a Zulu Nation DJ, "You played that day and if you made a tape, that tape would circulate and that's how good you were—determined by how wide your tape circulated. I mean, we had tapes that went platinum. That was before we were even involved in the music industry." That involvement was still years away, when Bambaataa would link up with entrepreneur Tom Silverman to release "Jazzy Sensation." In 1982, the cosmic hit "Planet Rock" by Bam with Soulsonic Force established Silverman's Tommy Boy Records as a contender and kicked off the electro-funk revolution—a sound that later resurfaced in the work of popular electronic outfits like the Chemical Brothers and Fatboy Slim.

The Birth of a Style: Techniques and MCs

Meanwhile, back in the Bronx, the hip hop virus was spreading like the plague, largely thanks to the efforts of Grandmaster Flash. . . . With . . . the supreme hand-eye coordination that earned him his nickname, Flash soon surpassed Herc in skill and popularity, drawing crowds and spinning breakbeats with unmatched speed and precision.

Flash and his crew also get credit for several other hip hop innovations. Young Theodore Livingston, the brother of Flash's partner Mean Gene, accidentally invented the art of the "needle-drop": Where Flash would have to physically spin a record back to find a certain spot, Theodore could do it by sight. Later he would expand on Flash's "quick-mix" theory by taking a record and making a rhythm using one record at a time. While cuing up a record, Theodore discovered that the potentially annoying noise of a needle working back and forth could be used rhythmically—what later came to be known as "scratching." Flash, of course, perfected these skills, and used them to wow audiences at clubs like the Back Door in the Bronx, his first regular venue. Here he also debuted the "beat box," a manually operated drum machine (by an English company called Vox) with which he would play a drum part in time with the track.

Flash was also at the center of another revolutionary change to the art form: the use of MCs to fully augment the musical entertainment. He came with not one, not two, but *five* MCs. What started out as simple catchphrases like "Say 'Ho,'" "Say 'Oh yeah,'" and "Clap ya hands to the beat, y'all" chanted over the groove was honed by Grandmaster Flash's Furious Five MCs, which included Cowboy (Keith Wiggins), Melle Mel (Melvin Glover, Flash's first recruit), Kid Creole (Danny Glover), Scorpio (Eddie Morris), and Rahiem (Guy Williams). Through the efforts of the Furious Five, MC-ing progressed to a whole new level with such complicated routines as back-to-back rhyming, in tandem flows, and choreographed moves. The Furious Five had a way of breaking up phrases to "make 5 MCs sound like one." MCs quickly reached the status of black ghetto superheroes with their strange monikers, outlandish outfits, and lyrical dexterity.

By 1978, MCs had stolen the spotlight from the DJs because they spoke directly to the crowd, making the experience of dancing to recorded music more exciting and live. Following the lead of Flash and the Furious Five, some of the more popular crews to emerge during this time were Grand Wizard Theodore and the Fantastic Five, DJ Breakout and the Funky Four (who later added one of the first female MCs, Sha Rock, and recorded the smash hit "Body Rock"), and the Treacherous Three, whose most famous member, the quick-tongued Kool Moe Dee, went on to a successful solo career. The MC became a true personality, like popular uptown trash talkers DJ Hollywood and Eddie Cheeba, who catered more to the disco crowd.

Before moving downtown to clubs like Danceteria, Negril,

and the Roxy in the '80s, rap developed its own venues to accommodate the masses that were coming out to shows. Though places like Harlem World (on 116th and Lenox), Disco Fever (in the shadow of Yankee Stadium), and the T Connection (on Gun Hill and White Plains Roads in the Bronx) no longer exist, they remain legendary.

Up from the Underground

One of the groups to bridge rap's transition from the underground to mainstream success was the Bronx's Cold Crush Brothers—Jerry D. Lewis (JDL), Almighty KayGee, Charlie Chase, EZ AD, Grandmaster Caz, and DJ Tony Tone. Formed in early '79, Cold Crush elevated the game with singing and chanting routines that expanded on the Furious Five's innovations. They gained almost instant respect, as a line from one of their famous routines attests: "We're bad one-on-one/Rock any MC pup and all hell breaks loose when we team up."

Of those innocent times, JDL says, "It wasn't about gettin' paid and all that, it was about something you loved, something we did from the heart. If you doin' something you love, you gonna do it to the best of your ability. Back then, groups were always tryin' to be extravagant and do things out of the ordinary."

At one point, Cold Crush was managed by Henry "Big Bank Hank" Jackson, a part-time bouncer who also worked at a pizzeria in Englewood, New Jersey. One day, while rapping along to a show tape of Cold Crush, Hank was approached by Sylvia Robinson, a former R&B singer who ran several independent labels with her husband, Joe. Sylvia had recently become interested in rap after a visit to Harlem World, and she asked Hank if he was interested in joining a rap group she was putting together. Though he wasn't an actual MC, he agreed, and went back to Grandmaster Caz for help.

Caz recalls giving Hank his book of rhymes, no questions asked. "I figured, if you get put on, you put us on," says Caz. "As you can see, it didn't work like that." The track that Hank recorded with Michael "Wonder Mike" Wright and Guy "Master Gee" O'Brien, using Caz's rhymes and Chic's backing track, turned out to be the monster hit "Rapper's Delight." Almost overnight, the trio, now called the Sugarhill Gang, became superstars, and the Sugar Hill label became the first rap powerhouse.

Caz, who received neither credit nor compensation for "Rapper's Delight," says, . . . "['Rapper's Delight'] didn't really represent what MC-ing was or what rap and hip hop was." But for the rest of the world, beyond the Bronx and outside of New York, rap had arrived. And 20 years later, propelled by the vibrant and dynamic urban culture of hip hop, it hasn't stopped moving and grooving yet.

Rap as Blacks' Response to Disco

Alex Ogg with David Upshal

Thanks to pioneers such as DJ Kool Herc, the Sugar Hill Gang, and Fab 5 Freddy, rap emerged while disco music was on the decline. Instead of the elite discos that primarily catered to wealthy white clients, the urban street was rap's early arena, and the music spoke both to and from a black urban experience that was rapidly taking shape as the b-boy culture of break dancing. Alex Ogg is the author of *The Guinness Book of Rap*. David Upshal is the producer and director of *The Hip Hop Years* in the United Kingdom.

FREDERICK BRAITHWAITE STARTED OUT AS A graffiti artist working along the Lexington Avenue line with the Fab Five crew—hence his *nom de plume* Fab Five Freddy. Before working as a promoter, recording artist and later a TV presenter, he witnessed some of the earliest DJ parties.

'I was part of the disco era. This is disco before it became commercial disco, when it was underground. DJs giving parties in schools, at restaurants that they would take over at night and they would simulate "posh" clubs. That scene, those particular DJs that played what was then known as disco, those guys inspired the generation that became the pioneers of hip hop. So I was around as the transition took place in the mid-70s.'

That transition involved disenfranchised black youths reclaiming music from untouchable star musicians whom they could no longer readily identify with.

'Let's say a group like Earth Wind & Fire—that particular

■

Excerpted from *The Hip Hop Years: A History of Rap*, by Alex Ogg with David Upshal (New York: Fromm International, 2001). Copyright © 2001 by Alex Ogg. Reprinted with permission.

time, they were wearing elaborate, gaudy costumes. It was something that seemed very far away from what a ghetto kid on the street could realistically hope to attain, or be part of.'

Disco had left many urban black kids behind. Its celebrity-strewn mecca, Studio 54 [an exclusive New York City disco], could just as well have been on another continent. Impresario Michael Holman saw this desire for ownership of an indigenous music and the frustration with vacuous records produce a climate similar to the one which engendered punk. However, he empha-sises the fact that peer group acceptance took several years.

'The people in the neighbourhood were into the artists who were coming out of California and from other places. Lo-cal groups and local rap artists who were rapping over turn-tables in the park were not quite that popular, especially with the older people from, say, mid-twenties up.'

Where punk had been a year zero explosion, hip hop was built block by block over several years, devouring its immedi-ate past rather than ridiculing it. Disco was its most recent an-tecedent and provided a fertile gene pool. However, many other early hip hop jams and record releases employed rock signatures and percussion effects rather than dance music, be-cause it was too 'soft' to freestyle over.

Before hip hop finalised its blueprint, disco kids in the Bronx were already hooked on the breakbeat sections the DJs would emphasise, as Fab Five Freddy recalls.

'When these particular records would come on, they would give a real interesting vibe to the party. The atmos-phere, the energy would change. Kids that knew how to break-dance would start dropping to the floor doing these crazy moves. This is before things had names and titles so it wasn't breakdancing and it wasn't hip hop, it was just energy.'

Fab Five Freddy notes that the development of a cultural alternative to disco was at least partially inspired by working class blacks being excluded from the mainstream.

'When you would go to these disco parties, particularly when they were given in the cities, or at colleges. The crowd was primarily a college crowd. They would sometimes put on the flyers: "No sneakers". That would be a reference to what you could say was the hip hop kid, or the real urban founda-tion type of kid.'

My Adidas—Hip Hop Fashion Statements

The sneaker was becoming an item of almost mythical importance to breakdancers, according to Michael Holman. Woe betide anyone who stepped on the toes of the early B-boys.

'Back in the old days of hip hop, the sneaker of choice would be shoes that would be actually old school even then. They would have been ten-year-old styles, like the plastic shell toe, the shell-toed Adidas sneakers. These were kids who, what they owned was on their backs and on their feet. So when you talk about sneaker etiquette, or sneaker intrusion, you're talking about this idea of, God forbid, you were to step on someone's sneakers. I don't know how they did it, but you would keep your sneakers spotless. Absolutely clean. And you're going through the subway system, you are going through New York City—it's not one of the cleanest cities in the world. How they would keep them clean I have no idea. Stepping on someone's sneakers could easily be a death sentence.'

Some of the more interesting fashion statements were made by combining sneakers with exotic sportswear—sailing and skiing apparel—sporting activities that were way beyond the wearer's economic compass.

'That has always been part of black fashion, mocking them [affluent whites], mimicking it, taking that fashion and turning it into their own.'

Despite the confluence of areas like breakdancing, graffiti and music, the embracing of hip hop as an umbrella term was still some way down the line, according to Fab Five Freddy.

'There really was no comparison, there was no analogy. There was no four elements of hip hop at this point in time. Basically, you had graffiti going full steam, completely independent of what was going on in hip hop for the most part.'

Watch the Closing Doors—the Graf Squad

Graffiti had decorated urban trains in New York since the early 70s. The origins of this DIY impressionism, or 'guerrilla art,' are variously credited to Greek teenager TAKI 183 and Jean-Michel Basquiat, aka Samo, though territorial wall markings were a fixture of New York's urban environment in the previous decade. In the 70s they simply grew in size and ambition, often bedecking whole tenement walls as well as subway trains. This threw the authorities and graffiti artists into a headlong confrontation that is still smouldering today on several continents. Fab Five Freddy was one of graffiti's earliest adherents and advocates. According to his observations, its growth sprang from a quest for identity and recognition common to all hip hop's constituent forms.

'Graffiti artists come up with another name, another persona, paint it all over the city on the trains and everything and—"Hi! That's me! I'm just as big as an ad for Marlboro cigarettes or Coca-Cola or any other big product."'

Michael Holman first came to New York in 1978 to work on Wall Street as a credit analyst. But he immediately became infatuated with the subway graffiti that decorated his route to work.

'I would get in the subway, about to get on a train, and these trains would go by with these amazing burners, graffiti burners, multi-coloured name tags. They would take up the whole train and I would watch them go by and just think, my God, this is amazing. Other people on the platform—do you see this? And they were all sort of in their own world and not even noticing. I guess it was all old hat to them and just boring vandalism and I was just shocked. It was the first tug, the first pull into that subculture.'

Like Fab Five Freddy, Holman believes that the different strands of hip hop—graffiti, breakdancing, DJing and MC-ing—were only considered as a collective entity some time after the event.

'It never really plays out the way you think it would in a neat package that historians would like to see it. There wasn't at that time anybody saying, "OK, this is like a hip hop happening." No one was saying that, because it wasn't that yet.'

At this stage, the dominant persona in this new culture was the DJ.

'It really is important to note that the DJ was truly the important artist then. It wasn't the MC, it was the DJ who made the party happen. It was the DJ who was the producer, who was the one supplying the soundtrack for the breakdancers and for the B-boys.'

However, some loose movement was definitely stirring, signified as much as anything by a new dress code.

'It was slowly becoming apparent to everyone uptown and downtown that this was something like the rock 'n' roll of the 60s, which had its own look, style, fashion. This was a subculture that had its own fashion, dance, aesthetic, music, lexicon if you will.'

It wasn't subtle, but Big Bank Hank of the Sugarhill Gang credits [DJ Kool] Herc with creating a compelling distraction from the turmoil of inner-city life.

'You could hear his system, with no exaggeration, three blocks away. He had a countless number of speakers, bass bottoms, subs, mid-range, tweeters. And he'd hook up—they'd plug into the street lamps. Lights would go dark from how much power was being drawn and the parties that he would throw. Oh, man, it was like something you'd see at the Superbowl. It was people losing their mind and no violence, and that was the key—no violence. To have that many people together and nobody wanted to fight. Nobody wanted to shoot. Everybody going home safe.'

MTV Brings Hip Hop to the World

Josh Tyrangiel

Since its inception in 1981, MTV has arguably been one of the most important factors in determining musical taste and setting trends in entertainment, style, and fashion for contemporary youth culture the world over. MTV has been equally important in the expansion of hip hop's popularity by bringing rap music and hip-hop style directly into America's homes. Yet while rap is now a staple of MTV's basic video rotation and rap acts regularly dominate taste-making shows such as Total Request Live, author Josh Tyrangiel, a former writer and segment producer for MTV News, demonstrates that this was not always the case.

THE HISTORY OF MUSIC VIDEO BEFORE MTV IS like the history of newspapers before the printing press; there were a few, but not many people saw them. As far back as the 1930s, musicians and avant-gardists were making visual accompaniments to music, and in the '60s, the Beatles, the Who, and the Kinks frequently made promotional movies to go along with their singles. When cable television became a nationwide reality in the early '80s and people suddenly had more channels than programmers could fill, music video was an idea whose time had come.

MTV lost tens of millions of dollars its first year, 1981, but its impact on visual culture was instant and permanent. Music could be absorbed visually—a concept that would have been

■

Excerpted from "Hip Hop Videos," by Josh Tyrangiel, *The VIBE History of Hip Hop*, edited by Alan Light (New York: Three Rivers Press, 1999). Copyright © 1999 by VIBE Ventures. Reprinted with permission.

incomprehensible just a few years before. More important to the industry folk, music could be *marketed* visually. Viewers were so sated by the eye candy that few realized they were watching three-minute ads furnished by a record label selling their new brand—um, band. Although the channel was initially available in just 15 percent of American homes, advertisers realized MTV was consistently delivering the right viewers: 12- to 34-year-olds with open minds and open wallets.

The Color Divide: Getting Black Artists on MTV

Amid a stream of glowing press, it took nearly two years for critics to recognize that there was something missing on MTV. "The program can be watched for hours at a time without detecting the presence of a single black performer," noted the *New York Times* in 1983. "MTV seems curiously intent on returning the black musician to the status of 'invisible man.'" *Rolling Stone* observed that of the 750 videos MTV showed during its first year-and-a-half on the air, fewer than two dozen featured black artists.

"Our research showed quite simply that the audience for rock music was much larger," explained then-MTV president Bob Pittman back in 1983. "The mostly white rock audience was more excited about its music than the mostly black audience was about its music—rhythm and blues, or disco, or whatever you want to call it."

At the time, MTV's most visible black presence was video jock J.J. Jackson. "MTV is a rock and roll station," said Jackson in a 1983 interview. "You think Donna Summer, Prince, and Rick James are rock and roll? I don't. . . . Someone has to decide what the cutoff point is going to be. And people who don't agree with that particular cutoff point are going to be a little angry."

On a 1983 edition of *Nightline*, an eloquently pissed-off Rick James took his cause to the airwaves. "Why should I, as a black artist in America today, spend good time and money on a video, when the biggest forum for music video in the world won't even play it? It's a real drag for me, man, and the only reason I keep complaining is that it's so important. I know I have white fans as well as black fans—I see them at my shows. The thing is, they shouldn't call themselves 'MTV: Music

Television.' They should call themselves 'White Rock TV' or something.". . .

Black Acts Change the Face of Music Video

It's not as if there weren't successful models of how to program black music video. BET [Black Entertainment Television] started airing R&B videos on its 90-minute show *Video Soul* in 1981, although the network fled when rap arrived just a few years later. WTBS created the highly acclaimed *Night Tracks* in 1983, which mixed black music with clips from rock and country acts. *Night Tracks* admitted to basing its content on watching MTV, and then doing more or less the opposite. Late-night video shows cropped up in many of America's big cities in the early '80s—WABC's *New York Hot Tracks* show-cased black talent and was a huge success. But none of them had what MTV had—24-hour airtime and built-in access to the country's most impressionable consumer audience.

In 1983, it was rumored that MTV wasn't going to play Michael Jackson's "Billie Jean" video because the music and vi-sual content were "inappropriate" for the channel's demo-graphic. As industry legend has it, then-CBS Records presi-dent Walter Yetnikoff phoned MTV's Pittman and told him that refusing Jackson's song would result in no more videos from CBS artists. "Billie Jean" was accepted, and *Thriller*, which had already sold three million copies to that point, sud-denly took off into the sales stratosphere.

Michael Jackson would be MTV's signature act for almost a decade, and his arrival cracked MTV open to R&B. After Lionel Richie and Billy Ocean took turns stinking up the medium, Prince swooped in and made sure R&B and MTV would stay together. His videos for "1999" and "Little Red Corvette" didn't get much play, but the sultry appeal of 1984's "When Doves Cry" was undeniable. *Purple Rain*'s five videos chipped away at MTV's programming conceit until R&B was no longer a stepchild, clearing the path for everyone from Sade to Bobby Brown.

The First Rap Videos

As MTV was slowly warming up to black music, though, black music changed. By 1986, rap was center stage—and if MTV worried how viewers would respond to Rick James in 1983, imagine what they thought when faced with leather-clad, gold-draped Run-D.M.C. just three years later.

In early 1986, Rick Rubin and Def Jam partner Russell Simmons were looking for a way to get Run-D.M.C. into the suburbs. They asked Aerosmith's Steven Tyler and Joe Perry if they would collaborate on a rap cover of "Walk This Way" with Run-D.M.C., and Tyler and Perry, at career rock-bottom, agreed, and also said yes to a video. All went according to plan, and the addition of mainstream rockers opened previously closed doors at radio stations and at MTV. It also helped that Rubin and Simmons delivered the video to MTV; Rubin was an NYU grad with MTV connections, and Simmons's combined skills as diplomat and salesman were unmatched in the industry.

"Walk This Way" was hip hop's first video classic. Aerosmith and Run-D.M.C.—separated by a wall—play their own versions of the song each driving the other crazy, until they tear down the wall and jam. The irresistibility of the metaphor no doubt helped make the song a crossover hit, just as Rubin had hoped. MTV played "Walk This Way" to death. Around the same time the Beastie Boys' "(You Gotta) Fight for Your Right (to Party)" and "Wipeout" by the Fat Boys with the Beach Boys saw serious airtime too. What did all three videos have in common? White people—which no doubt helped set MTV at ease. But the videos were also united by strong visual images: Run-D.M.C. wore black leather, the Fat Boys were fat, and the Beastie Boys shot Silly String out of their noses. The songs were light, the visual identities instant, and they became MTV's first rap staples.

Other rappers who wanted time on MTV couldn't help but take notice. Colorful, breezy, and cartoonish videos by Salt-N-Pepa, Tone-Lōc, and DJ Jazzy Jeff and the Fresh Prince followed. The songs were engaging, if perilously close to novelty. Meanwhile MC Shan, Too Short, Biz Markie, Schoolly D, Ice-T, Kurtis Blow, Kool Moe Dee, and Big Daddy Kane were making videos, too, and submitting them to MTV. MTV's programming committee even accepted some of them, but acceptance doesn't guarantee airplay. The majority of '80s rap videos just collected dust in the library.

New Challenges: Marketing Rap on TV

The people running MTV weren't stupid. They knew rap was happening on the streets, and a fair amount of them even liked it. But corporations don't just give it up for a groove. L.L. Cool J and Public Enemy—both on Def Jam—were the only acts to hit the streets and MTV at the same time, in large part due to the persistence of Simmons and Rubin. Other videos existed in a vacuum. Either they lacked a label chaperone who knew how to massage MTV, or they were deemed too hard for the audience. With a few exceptions, rap was perceived as a minefield, and before MTV walked through it, they wanted advertisers to set the ground rules.

"Rap is identified by some as revolutionary," noted one ad executive in a 1987 *Adweek* article, "and the music can be threatening to clients. The biggest job we have is convincing the client that it's not race music and that the artists aren't necessarily angry." Rappers did their part by embracing consumerism in a way rockers never had. Run-D.M.C. loved Adidas and rapped about it, the Fat Boys rhymed about their favorite foods, and L.L. Cool J dropped more commercial brand names onto *Bigger and Deffer* than viewers could find in an hour of prime time. Rather than back away, advertisers were intrigued by a new crop of eager, ultra-hip pitchmen. Run-D.M.C. signed on to hawk Adidas, Kurtis Blow represented Coke, Kool Moe Dee and the Fresh Prince pitched Mountain Dew, while the Fat Boys actually spurned offers from Coke and Burger King—a decision they no doubt regret.

Rap Video Comes into Its Own

In August 1988, with advertisers on board, MTV decided to air a pilot called *YO! MTV Raps*. The first episodes appeared on Saturday nights and were hosted by New York scene legend Fab 5 Freddy Braithwaite. *YO!* proved so popular that within a few months the channel cleared its schedule for a weeknight edition hosted by Ed Lover and Dr. Dre.

Ted Demme, now a film director (*The Ref, Beautiful Girls, Rounders*), was the co-creator of *YO!* "For the first couple of years," he says, "Fab and myself and Ed and Dre basically programmed the show. We had a real sense of what was fresh and new. Like when EPMD first came out, we'd play it even though it wasn't on the pop charts. Thirty days later, the LP went gold. Back then we really didn't have any standards problems whatsoever. MTV just let us do what we were doing. The show was getting great ratings and really good press."

In its prime, *YO! MTV Raps* was the best video show of any kind ever on television. Rap acts who had never dreamed of being on MTV were suddenly dropping by the studio for an interview and introducing their own videos. There were live performances by L.L. Cool J, EPMD, Public Enemy, Grandmaster Flash, and Eric B. and Rakim, at the height of their powers. Sometimes the show left the studio and traveled across the country, with Fab seeking out each city's scene and explaining why it was different and important. *YO!* wasn't about rap culture, it *was* rap culture. Dre, Ed, and Fab were the real thing, and they loved the music so much that they didn't mind explaining it to those just tuning in.

Gangsta Rap Hits the Airwaves

As successful as *YO!* was, though, the producers soon found themselves on a short leash. "When N.W.A. came up and rap started to get gangsta, and guns started coming out, everybody got really scared," says Demme. "And suddenly MTV's standards went berserk." *YO!* continued, albeit a bit watered-down, but the gritty, contrary street music the show championed failed to be integrated into the rest of MTV's programming. With a clamor of angry voices predicting the riots in Southern California, and perspectives as diverse as the Native Tongues and BDP to choose from in the East, MTV retreated. By 1991, rap on MTV was becoming the exclusive domain of MC Hammer and Vanilla Ice. *YO!* would be tinkered with, revamped, and canceled; in 1999, there were reports that it would be reintroduced as *Son of YO!* . . .

By the summer of 1993, the popularity of gangsta rap was no longer debatable. With alternative rock already on the decline, MTV sensed it was missing something big and dipped its toe back in by playing videos from Dr. Dre's solo debut on Death Row Records, *The Chronic*. The response was tremendous. The video for "Nuthin' But a 'G' Thang" was a players' party, with Dre and his reed-thin protégé Snoop Doggy Dogg acting as the governors of good times, West Coast–style. The song was bangin', and because the MTV audience hadn't seen or heard anything like it, they flipped out. . . .

The video famine quickly became a feast. [Alternative music video channel] The Box was playing so much rap that many people thought it was exclusively a rap station. The diversity—whether owing to individual callers or jackers—was tremendous, too. Tupac, the Luniz, Wu-Tang Clan, and Mary J. Blige all got major spins. MTV stuck to the crossover stuff—Death Row, Ice Cube, Salt-N-Pepa, L.L., Cypress Hill, and of course, Coolio—but had expanded its R&B coverage with the creation of *Jams*, a smooved-out vid hour that long remained MTV's highest-rated video show. BET—even more conservative than MTV—stayed away from the hot stuff, but still, hip hop videos could now be found on three different cable networks, more than any other genre.

The New Generation: Hip Hop Video at the Turn of the Century

More play meant more videos, and the egress of a definitive hip hop video style. Unlike other musicians, who hid behind their instruments or hung in the shadows, hip hop acts had no time for false modesty. Hype Williams, a 27-year-old painter turned video director, became ruler of the medium by putting the artists [such as Missy Elliott and Busta Rhymes] in charge of concept and plot. His goal? To get the performers to reveal themselves through their fantasies. . . .

By getting performers to use video as a canvas for fantasy, directors Williams, Paul Hunter, Marcus Nispel, Spike Jonze, Brett Ratner, Lionel C. Martin, and others have effectively transported the "anything's possible" ethic of the music. We may not be seeing performers as they really are, but at least we're seeing them as they want to be, which can be just as revealing.

Video has forever changed the nature of crossing over. The listeners who remember where they were when they first heard "Rapper's Delight" (and now, their children) buy the music because the beats are thumping and the MC's got skills. They seek out hip hop radio and are always ready for new sounds. But much of today's mass market wasn't exposed to hip hop in childhood. For them, video is the primary means of en-tree to the culture. Seeing artists makes them easier to relate to, and, critical to any pop phenomenon, easier to imitate. Hip hop videos, better than videos from any other genre, deliver personality. After four minutes, viewers feel they *know* Busta the wild child or Puffy the tortured soul.

EXAMINING POP CULTURE

Blowing Up: The Rise of the Hip-Hop Nation

Pop Rap

Matt Diehl

Matt Diehl, a New York–based writer who has contributed to *Rolling Stone*, *VIBE*, *Entertainment Weekly*,
and the *New York Times*, traces the rise of the less aggressive—and, not coincidentally, vastly more lucra-
tive—brand of hip hop that came to be known as pop
rap. Due to the success of the sitcom *The Fresh Prince
of Bel-Air* and acts such as MC Hammer and Vanilla
Ice, both of whom were willing to incorporate pop
musical styles (usually as samples) into their music, a
more radio-friendly type of rap music began to dominate the rap music industry, much to the dismay of
hip-hop purists.

RETURN OF THE ONE-HIT WONDER. MOST PER-
formers aren't so candid about their careers, but that didn't
stop Young MC from using this phrase as the title for his 1997
noncomeback album. Then again, the record didn't alter his
one-hit wonder status, confirming his standing as yet another
"pop rap" casualty.

Young MC broke big in 1989 with "Bust a Move." The
song was an immediate hit, its title breaking out of hip hop
vernacular and into mainstream use to describe making a play
on a fly target of desire. The album it came from, *Stone Cold
Rhymin'*, subsequently busted a move of its own all the way to
double platinum, and Young MC copped a Grammy for his
nimbly humorous singsong rhymes. But despite his earnest efforts, Marvin Young ultimately joined a litter of other pop rap
refugees on the hip hop scrap heap.

Sure, everyone can sing the "Oooh, boy, I love you so/
Never, ever, ever gonna let you go" chorus from Candyman's

■

Excerpted from "Pop Rap," by Matt Diehl, *The VIBE History of Hip Hop*, edited by
Alan Light (New York: Three Rivers Press, 1999). Copyright © 1999 by VIBE Ventures. Reprinted with permission.

1990 "Knockin' Boots" (another hip hop phrase popularized by a Top 40 hit), but can you name another Candyman song? . . .

The history of pop rap obviously follows a bloody trail, and we haven't even gotten to Vanilla Ice or MC Hammer yet. But closer examination provides a more complex picture—a look at the charts of 1997–1998 reveals that pop rap's impact has hardly waned. During that period, Puff Daddy was the undisputed King of Pop, yet his approach recalls nothing more than that of MC Hammer back in 1990. Puffs "Can't Nobody Hold Me Down" bit Grandmaster Flash's "The Message" in a style that flows directly from Hammer's lift of Rick James's "Super Freak" hook for his breakthrough smash "U Can't Touch This."

So what do we mean by "pop rap," anyway? Most simply, the word *pop* (as in "popular") signifies music that's reaching for the biggest conceivable audience. For many rap fans, such an approach inherently means gentrification of hip hop—yet hip hop's original intent was always about sucking the biggest possible audience into its groove. When DJs like Kool Herc cut up vinyl in Bronx parks back in the '70s and early '80s, they were trying to move as big a crowd as they could. And in the late '90s, supposedly "underground" rappers still rhyme about getting paid, insulting their peers whose albums don't go gold or platinum.

What, then, lies at the core of pop rap's dubious status in the hip hop community? More than anything, its critics claim, such accessibility often denies the emphasis on invention that hip hop heads have been demanding since the earliest street battles. When MC Hammer did a near note-for-note cover of the Chi-Lites' "Have You Seen Her," it had little to do with Kool Herc's collagelike assemblage of beats and the dance floor vitality that stems from that mix; instead, Hammer got over solely on nostalgia for the source song.

Pop rap's relationship to ghetto realness also remains a volatile issue, in particular when hardcore fans can sense rappers sanding off their rough edges for the mainstream audience. This debate can inspire such passion that, in one celebrated incident, KRS-One and posse stormed the stage during a 1992 club performance by P.M. Dawn at the height of that group's Top 40 success; rap's self-styled teacher made no bones that yanking the mike from Prince Be was, in his own words, "the first time a believed-to-be-hardcore artist took a physical reaction to a believed-to-be-commercial artist.". . .

Rap Sells Out?

[Street credibility was not necessary for] D.J. Jazzy Jeff and the Fresh Prince, however. While the Philadelphia duo hailed from a heavily African-American-populated city and Jazzy Jeff had won many a DJ championship with his wheels-of-steel mastery, from their first hit, 1987's "Girls Ain't Nothing But Trouble," they turned off rap purists. Everything about "Girls" was too smooth, from its suburban subject matter to its melodic music (complete with a crossover-ready novelty sample of the *I Dream of Jeannie* theme).

The Fresh Prince phenomenon really took off, though, with "Parents Just Don't Understand," off the 1988 album, *He's the D.J., I'm the Rapper* (even the title seemed intentionally instructional, designed for an audience unused to hip hop vocab); that success, however, resulted in further questions about the pair's street cred. The vibrantly funky cut-and-paste invention of Jazzy Jeff's solo cuts on *He's the D.J.* . . . couldn't stem the indignation from the underground about "Parents": The middle-class subject matter was still there, the music more inoffensively slick than ever, and, in the song's colorful video, the Fresh Prince's broad, bug-eyed humor was seen by some as pandering to a more "universal" (i.e., white) audience.

The end result: Top 40 success, as well as dominance on MTV, a previously color-impaired arena where, other than Run-D.M.C., hip hop was hardly in heavy rotation. . . .

White Noise

What really worried hip hop purists, though, wasn't so much the Fresh Prince's legions of white suburban fans as it was Caucasians getting on the mike themselves. It seemed inevitable that white kids would start to bust rhymes, and, considering the history of rock 'n' roll, that it would result in huge success. When the Beastie Boys hit in 1987 with "(You Gotta) Fight for Your Right (to Party!)" all the elements were there: a Budweiser punk nihilism, rhyme styles that flaunted and emphasized white nasal speech patterns, and a stance that didn't make clear where the love of rap and the parody of it began and ended.

It was a tricky mixture, yet one the Beasties deftly pulled off: while many were horrified that their debut album, *Licensed to Ill*, became the largest-selling rap album ever at the time, they satisfied the hardcore heads with underground grooves like "Paul Revere." Furthermore, their "white" accents were in a way an honest admission that they weren't going to front that they were black, an effort that wasn't lost on the hip hop community. "You know why I could fuck with [the Beastie Boys]? They don't try to be black," said Q-Tip, who appeared with the Boys on their classic "Get It Together." "They're just themselves—not trying to be something they're not." Continuing to occupy a complex area in the pop consciousness, the Beasties expanded their sonic vision to became a creative force unbound by genre, resulting most memorably in their truly inspired, truly insane pop culture roller-coaster ride *Paul's Boutique*, so innovative it was virtually ignored when it dropped in 1989.

Unfortunately, few of the white rappers that appeared in the Beasties' wake followed their creative lead; those that duplicated—or even surpassed—their chart success landed squarely in the pop rap camp. The most notorious, of course, remains Vanilla Ice. A towering southerner with an Aryan chiseled jaw, he proved himself the Pat Boone of rap with his massive hit "Ice Ice Baby" in 1990. A sort of Caucasian MC Hammer in his crowd-pleasing mission, Vanilla Ice's *To the Extreme* album actually knocked Hammer's *Please Hammer Don't Hurt 'Em* out of the No. 1 spot, and the symbolism did not go unnoticed. When African-Americans complained about white rappers' cultural imperialism, Vanilla Ice made it painfully obvious, from his stiff rhyme flow and awkward use of rap slang (at one point he boasted how he strapped on his jimmy, thinking jimmy meant "condom" instead of "penis") to his appropriation of African-American college chants for "Ice Ice Baby"'s chorus. Following pop rap tradition, Ice also bit the song's hook wholesale off a huge hit—in this case, Queen and David Bowie's "Under Pressure."

Ice's success spawned many imitators; "Marky Mark" Wahlberg had the biggest commercial impact, bursting onto charts and MTV with his club-flavored 1991 hit "Good Vibrations." Wahlberg proved an especially easy target—his brother was a member of bubblegum brats New Kids on the Block, and his underwear modeling career didn't exactly enhance his credibility. Most problematic, however, was his persona as a lower-class Boston jailbird thug, an attempt at fashioning a white equivalent of N.W.A.'s ghetto-gangsta image that shattered when his involvement in a racially motivated assault surfaced.

Even those who criticized Caucasian rhyme superstars, though, often followed their example. 3rd Bass positioned themselves as the white rappers who came closest to ghetto credibility, dissing the Beastie Boys and Hammer especially hard. 3rd Bass stuck it to Vanilla Ice in 1991 on "Pop Goes the Weasel," even beating up an Ice impersonator (played by punk god Henry Rollins) in the song's video. "Weasel," however, copied Ice's method even as it dissed it—and became the group's biggest (and only) pop hit. Like "Ice Ice Baby," "Pop" snatched a chunk of a popular rock hit (Peter Gabriel's "Sledgehammer") and constantly repeated its gimmicky chorus. . . .

The Rap-Rock Link

White rappers weren't the only ones biting popular rock songs to connect with the crossover audience (although the Beasties may have started the practice on wax with 1985's "Rock Hard," which lifted the monster guitar riff from AC/DC's "Back In Black"). The Fat Boys confirmed their status as a color-blind party band in 1987 with a rap version of the Surfaris' surf-rock classic "Wipeout." It was Run-D.M.C., however, who would take the rap-rock merger to the bank. Their 1986 rendition of Aerosmith's "Walk This Way"—a collaboration with actual members of Aerosmith—pushed them from hardcore New York street purists to national spokesmen for hip hop who'd go on to play the same arenas Aerosmith toured in their heyday (the pairing also revived the then-moribund hard rock band's career, infusing them with a much-needed jolt of hipness).

In a sense, the new version of "Walk This Way" made a historical link: Run-D.M.C. claimed that the cover wasn't just an assault on the charts—they'd been rhyming over the Aerosmith track as a breakbeat for years, along with other rockhard grooves from the likes of Led Zeppelin and Billy Squier.

When they covered the Monkees' "Mary, Mary" on 1988's *Tougher Than Leather*, however, what was initially an inspired approach began turning into stale pop formula—albeit one that worked for others. Tone-Lōc combined his blunted party philosophy, subtly lewd lyrics, and lazy Cali [California] drawl with a sliced-and-diced bit from Van Halen's "Jamie's Crying" (courtesy of the Dust Brothers, future producers of the Beasties' *Paul's Boutique* and Beck's *Odelay*), resulting in the massive 1989 hit "Wild Thing." He applied this approach again to a snippet of Free's classic-rock hit "All Right Now" on "Funky Cold Medina"—and complained that "like Mick Jagger said, I can't get no satisfaction"—and nearly duplicated "Wild Thing"'s success. That was no mean feat, as "Wild Thing" had become one of the best-selling singles ever, at the time trailing only "We Are the World."

The root of the rap-rock merger's appeal has often stemmed from its novelty status, and the novelty hit has proven to be a pop rap mainstay. Even respected hip hoppers like Digital Underground (with "Humpty Dance") and Biz Markie (with "Just a Friend") cashed in this way, resulting in two of the most memorable, hilarious rap singles ever. P.M. Dawn took a more circuitous route to the novelty approach: On their trippy 1991 breakthrough "Set Adrift on Memory Bliss," they sampled a large chunk of Spandau Ballet's new-wavey ballad "True" to go with Prince Be's bugged-out ministrations. Coming after the volley of James Brown riffs of the late '80s and early '90s, this choice seemed at once utterly original and utterly commercial. Groups like US3 and Digable Planets made hip hop's nascent embrace of jazz less avant-garde and more user-friendly. Digable Planets turned stand-up bass and Q-Tip-inspired rhymes into pop hooks, while US3 raided the vaults of the legendary Blue Note jazz label for the smooth sounds powering their hit "Cantaloop (Flip Fantasia)."

Unfortunately, novelty rap records aren't always so inspired. Sir Mix-A-Lot's "Baby Got Back" and 2 Live Crew's "Me So Horny" mixed pop hooks and repetition with a cartoonish version of African-American sexuality. Songs like "Baby Got Back" brought these seemingly taboo, "exotic" aspects of "black" culture into the mainstream. Not surprisingly, such outsize stereotypes played well with Middle America—

making a lot of white frat boys feel "down" as they chanted its chorus during Spring Break.

MC Hammer

The pop rap juggernaut that changed everything, however, was Oakland-based MC Hammer's 1990 *Please Hammer Don't Hurt 'Em* and its flagship hit "U Can't Touch This." *Please Hammer . . .*, at ten times platinum still the best-selling rap album of all time, turned on an ingeniously simple formula: You can get hits by recycling other hits still fresh in the public consciousness, like the bedrock of Prince's "When Doves Cry" that drove the album's second smash, "Pray."

Hammer's entree into the big time spawned rap's greatest aesthetic controversy yet. He had some unlikely boosters—rap's foremost polemicist, Chuck D, publicly admired Hammer's business acumen, which he saw as a positive example. "You're supposed to sell out!" Chuck D told *Rolling Stone* at the time. "If you got fifteen tapes on the shelf, your mission is to sell. You ain't giving it away. So I can't get mad at Hammer for doing what he's got to do." Many, though, were aggravated by Hammer's pretested, predigested hits, as well as his emphasis on dancing and feelgood entertainment over rhyme skills.

Hammer exemplified one key difference between East Coast and West Coast rap: just as New York is the home of edgy independent movies and Hollywood that of slick entertainments, Cali rappers aimed to please the largest possible audience while the jazzbo-virtuoso New York rhymers were often more interested in demonstrating skills to their peers more than anything else. This approach didn't just apply to West Coasters like Hammer and Tone-Lōc, either; gangsta icons N.W.A. made no bones about wanting to live as large as possible. In addition, while their ghetto tales came from the streets of South Central L.A., they were presented in exciting, cinematic narratives that played like blaxploitation [black exploitation] action-movie blockbusters, making hard rap that much more accessible to a wider audience. . . .

The Rules Change

Hammer's lack of substance, however, would come back to hurt him, and not just in the rap community. Dropping the

"MC" from his name—in effect, symbolically cutting himself off from hip hop's roots—he released an unexciting follow-up, 1991's *Too Legit to Quit*, which was considered a disappointment despite reaching triple-platinum levels. His next album, 1994's *The Funky Headhunter*, entered a pop world where the rules had changed: The effortlessly raw gangsta funk of Dr. Dre's *The Chronic* was now the gold standard of both the underground *and* the pop charts. Hammer's attempts to catch up and "go gangsta" were laughable, about as "real" as Kiss makeup (although the minor hit "It's All Good" introduced yet another hip hop catchphrase into mass use). So did the epic rise and hard fall of this once-international superstar—and the rise of gangsta rap—kill pop rap?

Hardly. Ever heard of a guy named Sean "Puffy" Combs?

Before we get into the sprawling Puff Daddy phenomenon, however, let's explore some of the other avenues pop rap took as the '90s edged toward the millennium. At the beginning of the decade, Naughty By Nature took an approach that would impact Puff Daddy's Midas-touch methods. On tracks like "O.P.P.," Naughty carried all the hallmarks of pop rap, such as a central hook taken from a big pop hit (the Jackson 5's "ABC") and an insistent chorus that became a pop-culture slogan the way "U Can't Touch This" did. Naughty By Nature eluded the pop rap stigma, however, by combining these elements with MC skills on a par with Rakim and Big Daddy Kane.

And in terms of pop rappers keeping it real, no one did it better than Salt-N-Pepa [S-N-P]. A trio of def females who were discovered while working at Sears, they burst onto the pop charts with 1987's "Push It," an irresistible slice of electrofunk that didn't hold back its sexual metaphor in either words or rhythm. Since then, with songs like the positive, uplifting "Expression" and the saucy, in-your-face "Let's Talk About Sex," S-N-P stayed pop-friendly while staying true to themselves, subtly changing their game to reflect hip hop fashions—resulting in one of the most durable careers in hip hop history.

The '90s saw other pop rap trends, too. There was, of course, the kiddie-rap variety, epitomized by Another Bad Creation and Kris Kross, whose hooky 1992 single "Jump" and "Totally Krossed Out" fashions (i.e., clothes worn backward) didn't translate into career longevity. Then there were the variations on southern bass music that exploded into national hits. Burgeoning in places like Georgia and Florida, songs like Quad City DJs' "C'mon N' Ride It (The Train)," FreakNasty's "Da' Dip," B-Rock & the Bizz's "My Baby Daddy," and Ghost Town DJs' "My Boo"—with their irresistible exuberance and upbeat grooves—skyrocketed seemingly out of nowhere to dominate radio and the charts. In the best pop tradition, multiple versions of bass hits even appeared on the charts at the same time, unlike, say, the numerous answer records to "Roxanne, Roxanne," each response differing slightly from the last, bass records can often be obtained in nearly identical versions—witness 95 South's and Tag Team's dueling smash 1993 variations on "Whoomp!/Whoot! There It Is."

Puff Daddy

The icing on the pop rap cake, however, came with Sean "Puffy" Combs. To categorize Puff Daddy as a pop rap artist is a bit facetious, especially considering the swath he cuts across the pop landscape as a producer, . . . record company mogul, and, eventually, solo performer. But in many ways he utilizes what's become the conventional pop rap approach. Most tellingly, like Hammer, he is a self-admitted beat jacker whose main goal, besides making boatloads of Benjamins, is to get the dance floor moving; and like Run-D.M.C., he's not above going to crossover-friendly rock tracks for his hooks— "All Around the World" from his 1997 megasmash *No Way Out* managed to sample David Bowie's "Let's Dance" while also squeezing in Lisa Stansfield's "All Around the World" on the Notorious B.I.G.–rapped chorus.

Puff Daddy retains street cred, however, by investing nearly everything he does with some hardcore rap sensibility. The stamp of approval from his affiliation with the Notorious B.I.G., one of the most respected rappers ever, puts Combs above reproach in the hip hop community, giving him an integrity check he can cash anytime he needs it. Biggie, in fact, was the vessel with which Puffy perfected his formula, combining in him the best of both East and West Coast approaches. On the one hand, Biggie had the gangsta swagger of Ice Cube, as well as a flow and lyrical virtuosity—not to mention a raw Brooklyn pride—that impressed even the most jaded hip hop heads. Yet all this came over crowd-pleasing, obvious samples like the Mtume bite on "Juicy."

As Naughty By Nature did with "O.P.P.," Puffy realized that it's better to show where you're from, to let the crossover come to him, not the other way around. He began exploiting this tension in his invention of "hip hop soul" at Uptown Records as epitomized by Mary J. Blige and Jodeci, yet it was in applying these methods to hip hop that he found his gold mine—and, in the process, made it okay for real MCs to have big pop hits. Indeed, only recently has East Coast rap made peace with the concept of selling out and begun to match its West Coast counterparts in sales figures. . . .

Pop Rap Comes Full Circle

The Fugees both built on Puffy's success with Biggie and provided a newer model for him to follow. Though their first album, 1994's *Blunted on Reality*, barely dented hip hop's consciousness, when they dropped *The Score* in '96 it became a multiformat Godzilla that topped rap, R&B, *and* pop charts. The trio could have easily been another positive-yet-accessible rap act a la Arrested Development and Digable Planets—groups that, after one hit, seemed like the future, but instead quickly faded from memory. Indeed, the Fugees often followed pop rap's hit-making formula to a T: As with Hammer's "Have You Seen Her," their versions of Roberta Flack's "Killing Me Softly" and Bob Marley's "No Woman, No Cry" were straight-up covers with amped-up beats. However, the Fugees' remakes didn't rankle hip hop purists as Hammer's did—they felt more like organic evolutions out of their own influences than desperate chart stabs; they were also surrounded by idiosyncratic hip hop grooves and shouts of Haitian pride.

It's striking the fine balance between staying "real" and achieving mass appeal that Puffy manages so well. He's made straight-up pop rap acceptable again in the '90s—witness the return of Will "Fresh Prince" Smith into the hip hop universe. While Smith was becoming one of the most bankable film stars in the world, his status as a musical performer was up in the air; that changed in the summer of '97, when his inoffensive theme to the blockbuster *Men in Black* (riding on the catchy chorus of Patrice Rushen's "Forget Me Nots") became one of the year's biggest singles, followed by a return to making albums with *Big Willie Style* and its No. 1 smash, "Gettin' Jiggy Wit It."

If anything, pop rap has come full circle: Puffy protégés the Lox continued the populist rap-rock lessons taught by Run-D.M.C., turning a rock hit like Rod Stewart's "Da Ya Think I'm Sexy?" into the 1998 crossover gambit "If Ya Think I'm Jiggy." Even "Marky Mark" Wahlberg was born again as a neo–De Niro in indie hits such as *Boogie Nights*. On the other hand, Puffy's example has allowed stylistic nonconformists like Busta Rhymes and Missy Elliott to succeed primarily by being themselves: indeed, Busta's "Put Your Hands Where My Eyes Could See" might have the most African rhythm (even if it is sampled from a Seals & Crofts record) ever to grace the pop charts. In the end, Puffy's machinations have metamorphosed him into a ghetto superhero that both Middle America and his homies can appreciate. By allowing everyone to see themselves in his success, Puff Daddy, no one-hit wonder, has dodged the career-killing bullet that zapped Hammer and so many of his pop rap brethren.

Rap: A Capitalist Tool

Nelson George

Cultural critic and longtime hip-hop insider Nelson George considers the impact of the commercialization of rap on the music itself and on the black and white audiences to which it was—and continues to be—marketed. George writes both a history of how the rap music industry developed into a dominant youth culture and an impassioned critique of the negative effects that capitalism can have on urban cultural expression and the communities it influences.

HIP HOP IS NOT A POLITICAL MOVEMENT IN THE usual sense. Its advocates don't elect public officials. It doesn't present a systematic (or even original) critique of white world supremacy. Nor has it produced a manifesto for collective political agitation. It has generated no Malcolm X or Dr. [Martin Luther] King. It has spawned no grassroots activist organization in the order of the Southern Christian Leadership Conference, the Black Panther Party, NAACP [National Association for the Advancement of Colored People], or even the Country Music Association.

Hip hop has actually had surprisingly little concrete long-term impact on African-American politics. It has made its mark by turning its listeners onto real political icons (Malcolm X), radical organizations of the past (the Black Panthers), and self-sufficient operations of the present (the Nation of Islam). It spread the word about the evils of apartheid. It articulated and predicted the explosive rage that rocked Los Angeles in

■

Excerpted from *Hip Hop America*, by Nelson George (New York: Viking, 1998). Copyright © 1998 by Nelson George. Reprinted by permission of Penguin Putnam, Inc.

1992. It has given two generations of young people a way into the entertainment business and an uncensored vehicle for expression. Chuck D once said he hoped Public Enemy would spawn thousands of black leaders. To the degree that his band opened the eyes of its listeners to political thought, Chuck D and his crew have probably affected many more young people than that.

Hip hop's major problem as a political movement is that MCs are not social activists by training or inclination. They are entertainers whose visibility and effectiveness as messengers are subject to the whims of the marketplace. For all Public Enemy's impact—and there were at least four years when the band embodied the best of this culture—its ultimate strength lay in making and selling records.

But this doesn't mean there has been no political impact from hip hop—far from it. From the Chuck D–designed b-boy in a gun sight logo to the Muhammad Ali–Drew "Bundini" Brown [Ali's trainer] interplay of Chuck and Flavor Flav, from the Security of the First World's onstage brandishing of toy Uzis and militaristic garb to the Bomb Squad's bombastic aural attack, Public Enemy made politics seem cool. In the process they also made politics a commodity. To be sure, this was a marketing tool with a wider purpose but, in effect, it was no different than what L.L. Cool J did for romantic themes or N.W.A. did for gangsterism. In the great pop culture wave constantly rippling across our shores, black nationalistic rap crested and, for the time being, has receded along with the career of P.E. and acolytes Paris, the X Clan, and others.

While hip hop's values are by and large fixed—its spirit of rebellion, identification with street culture, materialism, and aggression—it is also an incredibly flexible tool of communication, quite adaptable to any number of messages. That's one reason it has endured. That's why no one style has been essential for over three or four years at a time. That's why it has been so easy to turn every element of the culture associated with hip hop into a product, be it Tommy Hilfiger selling leisure wear, academics writing a thesis, breakfast-cereal makers hawking sugar-covered wheat, or presidential candidates seeking an issue.

Hip hop didn't became commodified in a simple, connect-the-dots manner. It morphed, like an alien in a sci-fi flick, to serve its different masters. Yet, unlike so many other underground cultural expressions, hip hop has managed to remain vital, abrasive, and edgy for two decades. The culture's connection to the African-American working and underclass, people usually without a media voice, enables it to communicate dreams and emotions that make outsiders uncomfortable. When even Sony Playstation features a gentle childlike rapper, it doesn't fatally undercut or mitigate the force of roughneck MCs like Mobb Deep or Wu-Tang. Somehow hip hop survives even the crassest commercialism or, at least, it has so far. . . .

Fat Laces

It was in 1985 that the athletic wear manufacturers began to see how the link between hip hop and their products could pay off big time—and, unsurprisingly, it was Russell Simmons [chairman of Def Jam Records] who made the connection real.

Run-D.M.C.'s "My Adidas" was a tribute to the seminal hip hop athletic shoe at the height of its appeal. Russell Simmons and his Rush Management team were determined to turn that record's message into money. Athletes regularly scored endorsement deals from athletic wear companies and Michael Jordan was already on his way to revolutionizing the marketing of sports gear with his landmark Nike deal. Russell wanted a piece of the pie for Run-D.M.C.

Run-D.M.C.'s 1986 headlining appearance at Madison Square Garden provided the right venue for Russell to prove his point. With several Adidas executives from Germany standing in the wings, Run-D.M.C. was rocking 20,000 New York b-boys and girls at Madison Square Garden. Before performing "My Adidas," Run told the crowd to hold up their Adidas sneakers. A sea of three-striped athletic sneakers emerged like white leather clouds over the heads of most of the fans. When Run walked offstage that night "the Adidas representatives told me that I would have my own line of Adidas clothing," he told the *Source* in 1993. "That was the most memorable event in my life" (at least until he became born again). Within a year, Adidas and Rush Management had negotiated a $1.5 million deal with the rappers to market Run-D.M.C. sneakers and various accessories, including a Run-D.M.C. jersey I still treasure.

With this deal a line had been crossed. Instead of just adapting existing styles and working with "found" materials, the hip hop community was now having things made expressly for them by major manufacturers. As a result, other deals were made. (Whodini made a small deal with Lacoste Sportif and L.L. Cool J a large one with Troop.) Happily, though, the creative energy was still soaring—evidenced when the next major trend emerged from the underground. . . .

Fashion Trends

The appropriation of high fashion items began in the late '70s with Cazals, a line of designer glasses frames that homeboys often wore without any glass as pure style. The Gucci and Fendi shift, in which ghetto designers used upscale logos mirroring the way rap producers sampled beats, took this game to another level. Once the taste for designer gear was whetted, Run-D.M.C.'s admonition "Don't want nobody's name on my behind" was history.

Old-school symbols of self-identification (nameplate belt buckles, stenciled T-shirts) gave way to the culture's total immersion, even obsession, with expensive status gear. Young urban adults and even teens became regular visitors to the Fifth Avenue stores of high-profile clothiers, occasionally intimidating customers and attracting the close attention of security guards. This shift, which would prove more enduring than hi-top fades, Lacoste Sportif sweat suits, and the Louis Vuitton logo on car seats, would be monitored by manufacturers large and small.

Homemade gang emblems drawn and spray-painted onto jackets and dungaree legs were part of the New York scene during the days [DJs] Bambaataa, Herc, and Flash were spinning in Bronx parks. Over ten years later another gang-generated style would rise out of the West. When the Oakland Raiders moved to Los Angeles in the '80s, their logo—a scowling pirate backed by crossed swords and the word "Raider" above his head—was adopted by kids in both of the city's major gangs, the red-garbed Bloods and blue-wearing Crips, as well as teens caught in between. The team's silver and black projected strength without declaring which "set" you were down with. Then the city's hockey franchise, the Kings, a team never known for its toughness, shifted from the blue and gold it shared with the basketball Lakers to the Raiders' silver and black. The Kings' revamped bold logo quickly became essential to the West Coast hip hop uniform, nicely complementing the boastful violence of the emerging gangsta style. In fact, N.W.A.'s original look—the Kings and Raiders paraphernalia, augmented by sunglasses called "Locs" and the stiff Dickies jeans and jackets—recast athletic wear in a new sinister light. In cities around the country gangs and drug operations gravitated to different sports merchandise. In New York, a Yankees blue cap with its white "NY" meant certain drugs were available. In Boston, one gang liked to wear the green and yellow parkas and caps of the Green Bay Packers.

Because gang members, particularly the more successful crack dealers, were so visible in the 'hood, the sellers of athletic apparel began courting them. When the new Air Jordans or the latest Chicago Bulls parkas were due in, retailers would get the word out to local dealers. These young dealers, many with romanticized views of themselves as outlaws not simple crooks, became tastemakers directing both their customers and neighbors toward new merchandise.

While the oversize parka and wool cap has been a hip hop cultural artifact for most of its history, the heavy winter boots as year-round attire flowed out of their use by crack dealers clocking on corners. In the tradition of appropriation that is integral to the scene, Timberland boots—high quality footwear worn by folks in New England and the Midwest for decades—suddenly became official urban style. Tims, as they were nicknamed, were for several years the Air Jordans of boots, they became equally ubiquitous in music videos, on stage, and in the streets.

While Tims-mania generated millions, its owners were clearly uncomfortable with the unexpected identification of its brand name with urban youth. When word of mouth of Timberland's lack of enthusiasm for the hip hop audience hit the streets (a message aided by Luggz and other competitors), Timberland disappeared from the culture as quickly as it had emerged as a staple. By 1996, the only ember left of the fire was that a top Virginia-based producer went by the tag Timbaland. Other than that, Timberland was as over in hip hop as the Sugar Hill Gang.

There are other stories of mainstream brand names reject-
ing an association with hip hop. In the early '90s, A Tribe
Called Quest's Q-Tip had several requests for Polo street wear
rejected by reps for the Ralph Lauren–affiliated company. The
stated reason was that they were worried how it would affect
the company's image. A few years later Lauren's operation had
turned a new leaf, using the defiantly dark Caribbean-
American visage of model Tyson Beckford to sell everything
from shades to underwear. Part of Lauren's reevaluation was
surely influenced by the astonishing marriage between hip hop
and Tommy Hilfiger. The elfin-looking American designer,
since his company's founding in 1985, had built a rep for making colorful, loose-fitting sportswear. Lacking the haughty veneer of Gucci or Chanel or the all-American aura of Ralph
Lauren, Hilfiger's brand was accessible in a manner similar to
the clothes early hip hoppers gravitated to.

Grand Puba, ex-member of Masters of Ceremony, some-
time-member of Brand Nubian, and the possessor of an in-
triguing off-kilter flow, has always been a hipster favorite,
largely because he has remained as much a cult figure as a
record seller. The lifelong New York–area resident once told
the *Source*, "If I only sold records in New York, you know, I felt
content with that," which was sweet to the ears of East Coast
true believers. So when Puba began mentioning Hilfiger's
clothes in his work, including during a guest appearance on
Mary J. Blige's *What's the 411?*, it served as a seal of approval
that led other rappers, industry figures, and active consumers
to make Hilfiger part of their wardrobes.

Around 1992 Puba and his crew, freshly dipped in Hilfiger
wear, encountered Tommy and his brother Andy just off a
plane from Hong Kong at JFK airport. Tommy didn't really
know who Puba was but Andy, a music fan, knew of the rapper's
music and his affection for their product. As a result of that
chance encounter, Puba and his crew were invited up to the
show room and given free rein to take whatever they wished.

Over the next few years Puba's endorsement and Hilfiger's
friendly response rippled through the culture. More MCs
wore clothes from the designer's Tommy jeans line, more MCs
mentioned "Tommy Hill" in rhymes (Q-Tip, Raekwon), and
more consumers, white and black, followed suit. Moreover,

Hilfiger, at his brother Andy's encouragement, began adapting his clothes to the hip hop–driven youth market. Since brand identification was such a powerful attraction, Hilfiger found that kids wanted his logos larger, more plentiful, and more colorful. Hilfiger accommodated them and this evolving style became known in the fashion biz as "urban prep," a way of dressing that took prep-school clothes and stretched them to fit the loose, baggy feel of '90s teen garb. Many young black designers were hired on to implement this change. One of Quincy Jones's daughters, Kadada, a hip hop tastesmaker who dated L.L. Cool J and later Tupac Shakur, became a free-floating asset for the Tommy line, dressing Michael Jackson in the gear for a *Vibe* cover, appearing in Tommy ads, and, for a time, formerly working for the designer.

A backlash against Hilfiger's sudden prominence resulted from a rumor that the designer dissed the black market on *The Oprah Winfrey Show*, a tale that took on the power of urban myth though no one could produce a tape on which he did so. The truth was (as is often the case) quite the opposite. Hilfiger, who initially knew little about hip hop, befriended Russell Simmons and Quincy Jones and became a strong supporter of *Vibe* through advertising and copromotions. In 1996, Hilfiger was the number-one apparel company traded on the New York Stock Exchange, due primarily to his embrace of hip hop and the large suburban audience excited by that urban prep look.

African-American Design Comes into Its Own

The amazing thing about the hip hop–driven growth of designers like Hilfiger and Lauren is that it did not drive smart African-American companies out of business. On the contrary, the entry of the bigger brands expanded the market and, in some ways, enhanced the position of the better designers. The larger brands not only made white kids more conscious of style, they made more adventurous dressers "keep it real" by seeking black designers. The Afrocentric impulse never totally died but, like everything else in this field, evolved into something else.

Instead of sporting Malcolm X T-shirts, many black and hip

white consumers decided they wouldn't be caught dead wearing the fashion equivalent of a Hammer record. In an economic manifestation of cultural nationalism, these consumers now buy their fashion black. Moreover, they are often rewarded stylistically since the black-run apparel enterprises tend to be more progressive in their choices of fabric, logos, and colors.

The greatest hip hop African-American fashion success story belongs to Karl Kani (Carl Williams), a Brooklyn native based out of Los Angeles. Karl Kani Infinity had estimated sales of $50 million in 1997, making the twenty-nine-year-old designer's operation the largest black-owned apparel firm in America. The road to this accomplishment wasn't smooth. When urban youth first adopted the jail style of baggy jeans damn near sliding off their butts, it was usually Kani's line that sagged around their ankles. Around 1991, he pioneered extra baggy pants and sweaters with his bold signature adorning each piece.

At that time, Kani's work was distributed in partnership with the Los Angeles–based Threads 4 Life–Cross Colours line, a brand known for baggy denim overalls highlighted by a garish red, yellow, and green logo. The teaming of black East and West Coast design aesthetics was unprecedented, as both managed to tap into urban taste and black pride. Ads for Cross Colours used to boast, "We want it understood that only Cross Colours is made by true brothers from the 'hood." As a division of Threads 4 Life, Kani's company generated $34 million in 1993. Later that year the bubble burst. Mismanagement and unpaid bills ground this combination to a halt and, to a great degree, opened the market for the Hilfigers of the world to move in. While the brothers who founded Cross Colours have yet to fully recover, Kani bounced back. After buying back his trademark name, Kani launched his new operation in November 1993 with $500,000 in the bank.

Kani's street rep was still strong. So was his design eye and his proven relationships with national retailers. Though no longer the newest, coolest line on the street, Kani managed to create an air of stability around him that, along with black businesspeople from the corporate mainstream, put him on the cover of *Fortune* magazine's August 1997 "New Black Power" issue. Since 1996, he has moved into couture, designing suits, slacks, and blazers. Around the country other innovative

African-American apparel companies have followed Kani's lead, people like Maurice Malone, ex-Mecca designer Tony Shellman (whose Enyce was funded by the Italian Fila company the way PolyGram backs Def Jam), Sir Benni Miles who successfully launched a line of nylon skull caps, and Fubu, a New York–based concern whose work exploded in the streets in early 1998.

Fashion Forward

Coming out of the first two decades of hip hop, there are two conflicting trends in fashion that, not coincidentally, speak to battling aesthetics within the overall culture. On the one hand is a coterie of slick, dressed-to-impress types whose embrace of high fashion names recalls the deification of Gucci and the like. Their signatures are the glitzy taste of Puff Daddy's Bad Boy camp, the late Gianni Versace's gaudy gear, and Foxy Brown's celebration of Dolce & Gabbana. In the past, the high stylers—the Dapper Dans of the world—were making uptown appropriations of the originals that were gleefully illegal and subversive. Now it just comes off as "I'm paid" consumerism with no subtext.

More encouraging are the folks who are holding on to the do-it-yourself philosophy that created hip hop. Chuck D has had his own clothing line, Rapp, for years, while Naughty By Nature and Wu-Tang both have stores and 800 numbers to receive orders. Russell Simmons has been slowly growing his Phat Farm out of his original SoHo location and L.A.'s expensive Fred Siegel boutique. Throughout the industry, rap entrepreneurs and local designers have been hooking up in hopes of building not just a Def Jam but a Kani-style enterprise.

I have no clue where hip hop style will go next, but the curiosity and ambition that have altered urban dress these last twenty plus years is nowhere near abating. While dollars will continue to be siphoned off by open-minded mass marketeers, the volatile nature of the culture means there will always be room for African-American entrepreneurs to innovate and, hopefully, build enduring companies. . . .

Bottle Bags and Soda Pop

As far back as I can remember, beverage companies have been hawking malt liquor in black neighborhoods. Colt 45 was the brew I saw consumed by parents playing spades at kitchen-table card games and by boys tossing cilo dice in schoolyards. It wasn't as disreputable as drinking cheap wine, as socially acceptable as Miller or Budweiser, or as upscale as cognac, but Colt 45 had its own cachet. It was the alcohol of choice for hard-living, macho brothers who took a cocky pride in brandishing the tall white cans.

When I was a teen in the '70s, Olde English 800 was on the rise. Colt 45 was your uncle's buzz; Olde E was younger and dumber. Its tall gold-and-brown cans promised a quick, intense high, which, if purchased right after school on Friday, would have you silly by sundown. But Saturday watch out. An Olde E hangover is brutal. If Colt 45 was an R&B brew, Olde E was old-school rap's favorite libation. It became as associated with Run-D.M.C. as black hats and Adidas sneakers. D.M.C. even penned a poem in praise of Olde E's charms: "Crack the quart, put it to your lip/You tilt it slightly and take a sip/Now by now you should know the deal/'Cause that one sip you already feel."

Back in the '80s, malt liquor in store-promotional posters either featured some macho double entendre slogan or a thick, scantily clad sister posed near the logo. Malt liquor ads never had the upscale veneer of cognac. ("I assume you drink Martel?" was one memorable ad line.) Nor did they aspire to the drink-it-at-ball-games-and-picnics appeal of Budweiser. Malt liquor was for roughnecks way before MC Lyte popularized the phrase.

Malt liquor ads had long used symbols of black macho . . . and music-driven spots on black radio. So it wasn't that surprising that a new brand seeking to woo the hip hop generation would employ MCs as spokespeople. What was remarkable was how shrewdly they hit their target. St. Ides ignored mainstream rap stars like L.L. [Cool J] or Heavy D. and went right for the hard core. The brew debuted out West with a radio spot featuring a chilly performance by King Tee, an Ice-T protégé who dragged a shotgun across the cover of his debut album. I thought his sixty-second St. Ides spot was actually better than his album. Certainly that spot received more exposure on black radio than anything the L.A. rapper would release on his own.

As the brew moved East so did its choice of rap spokesperson. A TV ad directed by *Video Music Box* host Ralph McDaniels featured members of the Wu-Tang Clan when the crew were still just underground heroes. Using King Tee and Wu-Tang sent a strong message to malt liquor's core consumers—St. Ides is for roughnecks like you.

Then St. Ides pushed the envelope. When they signed Ice Cube around 1991 to be the chief spokesman his street credibility was high, coming off his stellar performance in *Boyz N the Hood* and his *Kill at Will* EP. And for a time the St. Ides's crooked "I" logo and Cube were intertwined and inescapable in America's 'hoods. His trademark scowl hung in bodegas, grocery stores, and 7-Elevens, while his elaborate James Bond–styled TV ads rivaled his videos. The St. Ides marketing acumen and Ice Cube's visibility made the connection between hip hop, black youth, and malt liquor so uncomfortably intimate that Chuck D, rap's sometime policeman, commented negatively on the phenomenon in "1 Million Bottlebags": "They drink it thinkin' it good/but they don't sell it in the white neighborhood/How many times you see a black fight a black/After drinkin' a bottle/Or malt liquor six pack?"

Given how forcefully anti–malt liquor Chuck D was, it is strange that Cube appeared in a St. Ides radio spot that sampled the voice of Public Enemy's leader. Chuck D, rightfully pissed at this inappropriate appropriation of his work, sued St. Ides's distributor, the McKenzie River Corporation, for $5 million and made an out-of-court settlement that reputedly provided the down payment on an Atlanta home.

When Snoop Doggy Dogg ascended to the status of new hard-core hero, St. Ides replaced Cube with the Death Row [recording label] star. For his campaign, the brewers had a doglike caricature drawn of the MC that was employed to help introduce Crooked, a fruity beverage aimed at expanding the brand's base. So closely associated did St. Ides and Snoop's identification become that the same artist who did Crooked ads drew the scatological artwork . . . for Snoop's *Doggystyle*.

While St. Ides displayed a keen eye for the right hard-core rapper to push their brew, the makers of the benign, nonalcoholic soda Sprite have been equally shrewd. Sprite, once a poor relation to 7-Up with an undefined audience, began specifically targeting the hip hop audience in the mid-'90s. Wisely, the brand showed no interest in the roughneck approach. Instead, Sprite has gone for a less confrontational, more conversational approach. Its first TV spots featured music and images of A Tribe Called Quest. The colorful spots had a bright color scheme and trendy visuals that seemed aimed at adolescents and young women. The tag line for these spots was "Obey Your Thirst." Sprite then went to a more nuanced set of black-and-white spots that featured ex–Brand Nubian Grand Puba and the ex–Main Source Large Professor freestyling in a recording studio control room. The spots had an understated, soft sell feel—more like a documentary than an ad—that was aimed at rap connoisseurs, the kind of aware fan who knew who these two underground New York MCs were and would have been suspicious of a hard sell.

It was hip hop snob appeal, a bit of target marketing that Sprite would refine with a 1997 campaign updated with images from Charlie Ahearn's 1983 cult film *Wild Style*. Sequences from the original hip hop movie were restaged using contemporary stars (Nas and A.Z. freestyling on a Brooklyn stoop). By employing images from a film that never got wide release and is even hard to find on videotape, Sprite refined its rap snob appeal and displayed a deep understanding of rap's old-school history and that history's meaning for an active, smart segment of its consumer base. They even added more hip hop–oriented lines of copy: "Sprite has many styles 'cause you're stayin' true to what you do." I'm not sure it made Sprite an essential part of hip hop parties but it gave the product a connection with very cool aspects of the culture that certainly repositioned the beverage.

Rap Culture's Influence Is Pervasive

Russell Simmons, interview by Jane Spencer

Russell Simmons is a manager, entrepreneur, multi-media mogul, and cofounder of Def Jam Records. In this interview, Simmons argues that rap music and hip-hop culture have become so influential that they will mark how historians record the culture of the twentieth (and perhaps twenty-first) century.

THE MISSION WAS TO IMPROVE THE IMAGE OF hip-hop. A jumble of rap artists, industry producers, journalists, politicians, academics and spiritual leaders had assembled for what was billed as the Hip-Hop Summit, three days of discussions and press conferences about music and culture organized by rap mogul Russell Simmons, chairman of Def Jam Records. Guests included Minister Louis Farrakhan, Harvard professor Cornell West, and rappers LL Cool J and Sean "P. Diddy" Combs.

In the nearly three decades since rap was born, the music has emerged as a cultural force with a reach much broader than the black urban culture that created it. Now, 75 percent of hip-hop albums are purchased by white consumers, and the global market is constantly expanding. While the music is often celebrated for representing the gritty voice of the inner city, some performers come under fire from politicians, religious leaders and even fans for promoting misogyny, homophobia, profanity and violence in its lyrics. The rap industry is

■

Excerpted from "As Much as We Like Shakespeare, the Future's Going to Like DMX," by Russell Simmons, interviewed by Jane Spencer, www.newsweek.msnbc.com, June 15, 2001. Copyright © 2001 by Newsweek. Reprinted with permission.

fighting hard to fend off government regulation, and the summit included substantial discussion about self-regulation.

On Friday, after the rap stars and other attendees had dispersed, *Newsweek's* Jane Spencer spoke with Simmons about the summit—and the future of hip-hop.

NEWSWEEK: *There was a lot of discussion at the summit about media coverage of hip-hop—and the tendency to focus on violence, crime and gangsta rap artists. What stories are not being covered?*

RUSSELL SIMMONS: There's a lot of talk about rappers and their cars, rappers and their guns. There's no talk about rappers and their charities—and there are many. The rap community gives more back to their community than any music group that you can think of. [Queen] Latifah visits schools all the time. LL Cool J has Camp Cool J. Puff Daddy has Daddy's House. Y-Clef has the Clef Kids. Master P has a foundation. Some of the burden of the plight of their people falls on their shoulders, and they feel it more than other artists, but this stuff is not publicized. People leave that out. We forget that the biggest rapper in the world is Will Smith. The second biggest-selling-rapper is Lauryn Hill. There are so many positive rappers out there putting out records.

But there's a degree of reality to the violence, with the death of Tupac Shakur, Notorious B.I.G. . . .

If you look back over the 27 years of hip-hop, you have these two high-profile people that died. We still haven't caught either murderer. We don't actually know that either one is a rapper. They're convicted right away in people's minds. I'm not saying there's not a violence problem. Rappers don't become shooters. Shooters become rappers. These people come from this difficult environment and bring a lot of baggage. Just because they get a hit record doesn't mean that their life changes or that their mindset changes. A hit record won't transform someone overnight into a model citizen.

How do you respond to those who criticize the artists you produce for condoning violence and sexism in their lyrics?

People attack us from the outside. They don't listen close enough. I cannot condemn music that's a reflection of what happens in society. If an artist says f—k the police, that's fine by me. It's a protest song. The lyrics were clear on what they felt and why they felt. Sometimes I remind artists to say why they're saying it, even if the rap community may already know. That little bit may help people outside the community understand it as well. The messages are clear. They're about the realities these people face and the suffering under the conditions they live in.

Others have criticized hip-hop's celebration of capitalism and materialism.

The American dream is all the crap they sell you on television, and when you don't have it, it's much more attractive. That's part of what the artists are saying. People want what they see on TV. They don't want to be second class. The American dream is a theme of jazz and blues. Chuck Berry had an orange suit. He wasn't into ripped jeans. Elvis Presley had a ton of cars. They're rebelling because they hate what they're living and they want to buy into America. When you get these things, and you travel, they realize it's not everything. JZ says his Bentley just sits in the garage. Puffy's got a few Bentleys, but he rides around in his Volkswagen.

What about the role of women in the hip-hop community? There were some young girls at the summit who talked about how awful some lyrics made them feel.

The lyrics are a reflection of the sexism that exists in our society. I hope that this summit inspired more people to be respectful of women—and I hope that women are inspired to be more respectful of themselves. I don't want to judge them either—but Lil' Kim, and many women rappers are very aggressive. That's their response to very aggressive men.

One of the resolutions from the summit was a new commitment to the "Rap the Vote" project. What's the link between hip-hop and politics?

Kids fuel all the revolutions. Who do you think the Black Panthers were? What was Woodstock? Who's throwing rocks in Israel? Who really is adamant about their fight or struggle? It's young people. The FCC [Federal Communications Commission] is suing a radio station over an Eminem record. These are the kind of sparks that wake people up. The hip-hop community is going to mobilize. We plan to get the word out about candidates and issues like race profiling and rap profiling. We're compassionate, we're concerned about people that are suffering. We want some of the ideals that the Democrats—

and a few that Ralph Nader—talks about. Poor people should benefit from the success we've had.

What is it that makes the reach of hip-hop so broad? 75 percent of hip-hop albums are purchased by whites.

There's a real connection between the trailers and the projects. Kids reject racism. We have this great melting pot in America, and kids are working hard at turning the flame up on it. When you watch MTV, you see that. You can't use race as a reason to separate poor people who have the same issues with America. It's also the integrity in the music. All this gangsta honesty. This poetry is about a real lifestyle that people are stuck with—or fortunate enough to have, depending on the record.

Do you see the rawness—the violence and the profanity—as part of that honesty?

It's a reflection of reality. They want to break the glass, rather than change the society. The truth always has strong redeeming qualities—listening to the way people talk, understanding the way they think.

Do artists and the industry have a responsibility to deliver a larger message or a mission beyond merely reporting or reflecting the problems of the culture?

We talked a lot about how we might make that more part of the music. We said, "Let's watch the news and say what we think about it in the music." We hope that people will be inspired to take the lead and change, instead of just having so much about anger and frustration—which is an honest depiction of a lot of people's plight. But we said, "Let's talk about aspirations and possibilities." We want to do more of that. I think people see that there's that great opportunity. We hope that's what comes out of this summit. We want to remind people how powerful they are—and to celebrate that power, and then talk about all of their options, in terms of using that power. . . .

What will the new labeling requirements proposed at the summit actually change? Will increasing the visibility of warning labels about explicit content do anything to stop an 8-year-old from buying a CD?

What's to stop an 8-year-old from buying a book? Words are not regulated. It's not constitutional. Other industries can lobby and sell you anything. They can sell you cigarettes to kill. They have such strong lobbies they can get away with anything. And we can't even sell books—or lyrics, or language. That's crazy. This doesn't hurt you—this inspires you, or at the very least, gives you insight.

Conrad Muhammad [a Black Muslim minister who has strongly criticized Simmons and the industry for promoting violence] has suggested that as a producer, you exploit hip-hop for white audiences with "penny-chasing, champagne-drinking, gold-teeth-wearing, modern-day Sambos."

People wear gold teeth. White kids in projects wear them too. All those things he refers to are cultural subtleties that rappers have promoted. All these things become the language of the mainstream, the language of young America. The religious right criticizes it like they do any of the new ideas of how people dress, or youth language or culture. The way they did all the jazz artists, the blues artists, for the aspirational stuff, the sexual stuff. All that was perceived as terrible and is thought of as great today. Elvis Presley is even OK today. As much as we like Shakespeare, the future's going to like DMX.

Hip-Hop Nation

Christopher John Farley

Rap has changed in innumerable ways since its inception during the 1970s. In this article Farley, a pop music critic and staff writer for *Time*, contends that no matter what style or artist is at the forefront of popularity, rap's influence on music, fashion, film, advertising, and even politics shows that America has truly become a "hip-hop nation."

MUSIC MIXES WITH MEMORY. AS WE THINK BACK over the 20th century, every decade has a melody, a rhythm, a sound track. The years and the sounds bleed together as we scan through them in our recollections, a car radio searching for a clear station. The century starts off blue: Robert Johnson selling his soul to the devil at the crossroads. Then the jazz age: Louis Armstrong, Duke Ellington and, later on, Benny Goodman and "Strange fruit hanging from the poplar trees." Midcentury, things start to rock with Chuck Berry, "Wop-bop-a-loo-bop a-lop bam boom!" [Little Richard], the Beatles, Aretha Franklin, "a hard rain's a-gonna fall" [Bob Dylan], Bob Marley, Stevie Wonder. It might be better to forget the '80s—the posturing heavy-metal bands, Debbie Gibson, "Let's get physical—physical," [Olivia Newton-John], the guy with the haircut in Flock of Seagulls. Perhaps the remembered sounds of R.E.M., U2 and Prince can drown them all out.

And how will we remember the last days of the '90s? Most likely, to the rough-hewn beat of rap. Just as F. Scott Fitzgerald [author of *The Great Gatsby*] lived in the jazz age, just as Dylan and Jimi Hendrix were among the rulers of the age of rock, it could be argued that we are living in the age of hip-hop. "Rock is old," says Russell Simmons, head of the hip-hop

■

Excerpted from "Hip-Hop Nation," by Christopher John Farley, www.time.com, February 8, 1999. Copyright © 1999 by Time, Inc. Reprinted with permission.

label Def Jam, which took in nearly $200 million in 1998. "It's old people's s——. The creative people who are great, who are talking about youth culture in a way that makes sense, happen to be rappers."

Consider the numbers. In 1998, for the first time ever, rap outsold what previously had been America's top-selling format, country music. Rap sold more than 81 million CDs, tapes and albums last year, compared with 72 million for country. Rap sales increased a stunning 31% from 1997 to 1998, in contrast to 2% gains for country, 6% for rock and 9% for the music industry overall. Boasts rapper Jay-Z, whose [1999] album, *Vol. 2 . . . Hard Knock Life* (Def Jam), has sold more than 3 million copies: "Hip-hop is the rebellious voice of the youth. It's what people want to hear."

Even if you're not into rap, hip-hop is all around you. It pulses from the films you watch (seen a Will Smith movie lately?), the books you read (even Tom Wolfe peels off a few raps in his best-selling . . . novel [*A Man in Full*]), the fashion you wear (Tommy Hilfiger, FUBU). . . .

Hip-hop got its start in black America, but now more than 70% of hip-hop albums are purchased by whites. In fact, a whole generation of kids—black, white, Latino, Asian—has grown up immersed in hip-hop. "I'm hip-hop every day," declares 28-year-old Marlon Irving, a black record-store employee in Portland, Ore. "I don't put on my hip-hop." Says Sean Fleming, a white 15-year-old from Canton, Ga.: "It's a totally different perspective, and I like that about it." Adds Katie Szopa, 22, a white page at NBC in New York City: "You do develop a sense of self through it. You listen and you say, 'Yeah, that's right.'"

Hip-hop represents a realignment of America's cultural aesthetics. Rap songs deliver the message, again and again, to keep it real. The [twentieth-century German] poet Rainer Maria Rilke wrote that "a work of art is good if it has sprung from necessity." Rap is the music of necessity, of finding poetry in the colloquial, beauty in anger, and lyricism even in violence. Hip-hop, much as the blues and jazz did in past eras, has compelled young people of all races to search for excitement, artistic fulfillment and even a sense of identity by exploring the black underclass. "And I know because of [rapper]

KRS-1," the white ska-rap singer Bradley Nowell of Sublime once sang in tribute to rap. Hip-hop has forced advertisers, filmmakers and writers to adopt "street" signifiers like cornrows and terms like player hater. Invisibility has been a long-standing metaphor for the status of blacks in America. "Don't see us/but we see you," hip-hop band the Roots raps on a new song. Hip-hop has given invisibility a voice.

But what does that voice have to say?

Now tell me your philosophy
On exactly what an artist should be.
—Lauryn Hill, "Superstar"

It's a Friday night, early December 1998, and you're backstage at *Saturday Night Live*. You're hanging out in the dressing room with Lauryn Hill, who is sitting on the couch, flipping through a script. The 23-year-old rapper-singer-actress is the musical guest on this week's show. It's her coming-out party, the first live TV performance she's done since releasing her critically acclaimed and best-selling album *The Miseducation of Lauryn Hill*. She might also do a little acting on the show—SNL staff members have asked her to appear in a skit. But as Hill reads, her small rose-blossom lips wilt into a frown. She hands you the script. It's titled Pimp Chat—it's a sketch about a street hustler with a talk show. Hill's role: a 'ho. Or, if she's uncomfortable with that, she can play a female pimp. Hmmm. Now, being in an *SNL* sketch is a big opportunity—but this one might chip away at her image as a socially conscious artist. What's it going to be?

It's all about the Benjamins, baby.
—Sean ("Puffy") Combs
"It's All About the Benjamins"

You are in a recording studio in midtown Manhattan, hanging out with hip-hop superproducer Sean ("Puffy") Combs. It's 1997, and Puffy is keeping a low profile, working on his new album, his first as a solo performer. This album will be his coming-out party. He's eager to play a few tracks for you. People have him all wrong, he says. He majored in business management at Howard. He's not just about gangsta rap. Sounds from his new album fill the room. One song is based on a bit from the score to *Rocky*. Another, a sweeping, elegiac number, uses a portion of "Do You Know Where You're Going To?" That's what he's about, Combs says. Classic pop. "I'm living my life right," he says. "So when it comes time for me to be judged, I can be judged by God."

> You're mad
> because my style you're admiring
> Don't be mad—UPS is hiring.
> —The Notorious B.I.G.
> "Flava in Your Ear" (Remix)

Hip-hop is perhaps the only art form that celebrates capitalism openly. To be sure, filmmakers pore over weekend grosses, but it would be surprising for a character in a Spielberg film to suddenly turn toward the camera and shout, "This picture's grossed $100 million, y'all! Shout out to Dream-Works!" Rap's unabashed materialism distinguishes it sharply from some of the dominant musical genres of the past century. For example, nobody expects bluesmen to be moneymakers—that's why they're singing the blues. It's not called the greens, after all. As for alternative rockers, they have the same relationship toward success that one imagines [television character] Ally McBeal has toward food: even a small slice of the pie leaves waves of guilt. Rappers make money without remorse. "These guys are so real, they brag about money," says Def Jam's Simmons. "They don't regret getting a Coca-Cola deal. They brag about a Coca-Cola deal."

Major labels, a bit confused by the rhythms of the time, have relied on smaller, closer-to-the-street labels to help them find fresh rap talent. Lauryn Hill is signed to Ruffhouse, which has a distribution deal with the larger Columbia. Similar arrangements have made tens of millions of dollars for the heads of these smaller labels, such as Combs (Bad Boy), Master P (No Limit), Jermaine Dupri (So So Def), and Ronald and Bryan Williams (co-CEOs of Cash Money, home to rising rapper Juvenile).

"I'm not a role model," rapper-mogul-aspiring-NBA-player Master P says. "But I see myself as a resource for kids. They can say, 'Master P has been through a lot, but he changed his life, and look at him. I can do the same thing.' I think anyone who's a success is an inspiration."

Master P introduced something new to contemporary pop: shameless, relentless and canny cross-promotion. Each of the releases on his New Orleans–based No Limit label contains promotional materials for his other releases. His established artists (like Snoop Dogg) make guest appearances on CDs released by his newer acts, helping to launch their debuts. And his performers are given to shouting out catchphrases like "No Limit soldiers!" in the middle of their songs—good advertising for the label when the song is being played on the radio.

Madison Avenue has taken notice of rap's entrepreneurial spirit. Tommy Hilfiger has positioned his apparel company as the clothier of the hip-hop set, and he now does a billion dollars a year in oversize shirts, loose jeans and so on. "There are no boundaries," says Hilfiger. "Hip-hop has created a style that is embraced by an array of people from all backgrounds and races." However, fans are wary of profiteers looking to sell them back their own culture. Says Michael Sewell, 23, a white congressional staff member and rap fan: "I've heard rap used in advertising, and I think it's kind of hokey—kind of a goofy version of the way old white men perceive rap."

But the ads are becoming stealthier and streetier. Five years ago, Sprite recast its ads to rely heavily on hip-hop themes. Its newest series features several up-and-coming rap stars (Common, Fat Joe, Goodie Mob) in fast-moving animated clips that are intelligible only to viewers raised on Bone-Thugs-N-Harmony and Playstation. According to Sprite brand manager Pina Sciarra, the rap campaign has quadrupled the number of people who say that Sprite is their favorite soda.

Hollywood too is feeling the rap beat. After Lauryn Hill passed on a role in *The Cider-House Rules* (an adaptation of the John Irving book), filmmakers cast hip-hop soul singer Erykah Badu. Ice Cube, who has appeared in such movies as *Boyz N the Hood* and *Friday*, [stars] with George Clooney in the Gulf War thriller *Three Kings*. Queen Latifah, featured in the . . . film *Living Out Loud*, is now . . . the host of a TV talk show. And the former Fresh Prince, Will Smith, has become one of the most in-demand actors around. Ice Cube—who performed a song with Public Enemy titled "Burn Hollywood Burn" in

1990—says Tinseltown wants rapper actors because "we add a sense of realism where sometimes a trained actor can't deliver that reality the way it needs to be done."

Warren Beatty, who directed and starred in *Bulworth*, a comedy about a Senator who becomes possessed by the spirit of hip-hop, became interested in the subject because "it seemed to have a similar protest energy to the Russian poets of the 1960s. The Russian poets reigned in Moscow almost like rock itself reigned in the U.S. Ultimately it seemed to me that hip-hop is where the voice of protest is going in the inner city and possibly far beyond because the culture has become so dominated by entertainment."

Even Tom Wolfe, who documented the counterculture in the '60s and greed in the '80s, found himself buying a stack of hip-hop records in order to understand Atlanta in the '90s for his best-selling book *A Man in Full*. In several sections of his novel, Wolfe offers his own sly parodies of today's rap styles: "How'm I spose a love her/Catch her mackin' with the brothers," Wolfe writes in a passage. "Ram yo' booty! Ram yo' booty!" Most of the characters in *A Man in Full* are a bit frightened by rap's passion. It's Wolfe's view that "hip-hop music quite intentionally excludes people who are not in that world." That world, however, is growing. . . .

> We in the '90s
> And finally it's looking good
> Hip-hop took it to billions
> I knew we would.
> —Nas, "We Will Survive"

All major modern musical forms with roots in the black community—jazz, rock, even gospel—faced criticism early on. Langston Hughes, in 1926, defended the blues and jazz from cultural critics. Hardcore rap has triumphed commercially, in part, because rap's aesthetic of sampling connects it closely to what is musically palatable. Some of the songs hard-core rappers sample are surprisingly mainstream. DMX raps about such subjects as having sex with bloody corpses. But one of his songs, "I Can Feel It," is based on Phil Collins' easy-listening staple "In the Air Tonight." Jay-Z's hit song "Hard-Knock Life" draws from the musical *Annie*. Tupac's "Changes" uses

Bruce Hornsby. [Rapper] Silkk the Shocker samples the not-so-shocking Lionel Richie.

The underlying message is this: the violence and misogyny and lustful materialism that characterize some rap songs are as deeply American as the hokey music that rappers appropriate. The fact is, this country was in love with outlaws and crime and violence long before hip-hop—think of Jesse James, and Bonnie and Clyde—and then think of the movie *Bonnie and Clyde*, as well as *Scarface* and the *Godfather* saga. In the movie *You've Got Mail*, Tom Hanks even refers to the *Godfather* trilogy as the perfect guide to life, the *I-Ching* for guys. Rappers seem to agree. Snoop Dogg's sophomore album was titled *The Doggfather*. Silkk the Shocker's new album is called *Made Man*. On his song "Boomerang," Big Pun echoes [actor] James Cagney in *White Heat*, yelling, "Top of the world, Ma! Top of the world!"

Corporate America's infatuation with rap has increased as the genre's political content has withered. Ice Cube's early songs attacked white racism; Ice-T sang about a Cop Killer; Public Enemy challenged listeners to "fight the power." But many newer acts such as DMX and Master P are focused almost entirely on pathologies within the black community. They rap about shooting other blacks but almost never about challenging governmental authority or encouraging social activism. "The stuff today is not revolutionary," says Bob Law, vice president of programming at WWRL, a black talk-radio station in New York City. "It's just, 'Give me a piece of the action.'"

Hip-hop is getting a new push toward activism from an unlikely source—Beastie Boys. The white rap trio began as a Dionysian semiparody of hip-hop, rapping about parties, girls and beer. Today they are the founders and headliners of the Tibetan Freedom Concert, an annual concert that raises money for and awareness about human-rights issues in Tibet. [In February 1999] Beastie Boys, along with the hip-hop-charged hard-rock band Rage Against the Machine and the progressive rap duo Black Star, staged a controversial concert in New Jersey to raise money for the legal fees of Mumia Abu-Jamal, a black inmate on death row for killing a police officer. Says Beastie Boy Adam Yauch: "There's a tremendous amount of evidence that he didn't do it and he was a scapegoat."

Yauch says rap's verbal texture makes it an ideal vessel to communicate ideas, whether satirical, personal or political. That isn't always a good thing. "We've put out songs with lyrics in them that we thought people would think were funny, but they ended up having a lot of really negative effects on people. [Performers] need to be aware that when you're creating music it has a tremendous influence on society."

Sitting in the conference room on the 24th floor of the Time & Life Building, Kool Herc thinks back to the start of rap with a mixture of fondness and sadness. He'd like to see rappers "recognize their power, in terms of politics and economics." Hip-hop has not made him powerful or rich. "I never looked at it like that," he says. "I was just having fun. It was like a hobby to me." But he would appreciate more recognition. When he calls local radio stations, looking for an extra ticket or two for a hip-hop show, he's often told there are none available—even for the father of the form. Still, he's planning a comeback. . . . Says Herc: "Respect is due."

Friday night at Life, a dance club in lower Manhattan. Grandmaster Flash pulls the 11-P.M.-to-2-A.M. shift, and he's doing his thing. The Furious Five have long since broken up. Flash had drug problems, money problems and a court battle with his old record company, Sugar Hill, but he says today he has no ill will. He's the musical director on HBO's popular *Chris Rock Show*. And he's helping to develop a movie script about his life. "I was bitter a while back because I got into this for the love," says Flash. "I gave these people the biggest rap group of all time. But as long as there's a God, as long as I am physically able to do what I do—what I did—I can do it again."

The dance floor is getting crowded. Flash puts on a record. Does a little scratching. He plays the instrumental intro again and again and then lets it play through. "Ain't no stopping us now . . . "

> At first I did not know what I wanted. But in the end I understood the language. I understood it, I understood it, I understood it all wrong perhaps. That is not what matters. . . . Does this mean that I am freer than I was?"
> —Samuel Beckett, *Molloy*

In Mill Valley, Calif., in a one-bedroom apartment above a

coin-operated laundry, Andre Mehr, a white 17-year-old with a crew cut, and Emiliano Obiedo, a ponytailed 16-year-old who is half white and half Hispanic, are huddled over a PC. A beat spirals up. Obiedo offers some advice, and Mehr clatters away at the keyboard. They are making music. Once they settle on a beat, Obiedo will take a diskette bearing a rhythm track home and lay down some rhymes. Soon they hope to have enough for a CD. Boasts Obiedo: "I'm going to change rap."

Across the country, similar scenes are playing out as kids outside the black community make their own hip-hop or just listen in. Some say they don't pay much attention to the lyrics, they just like the beat. "I can't relate to the guns and killings," says Mehr. Others are touched more deeply. Says 15-year-old Sean Fleming: "I can relate more and get a better understanding of what urban blacks have to go through."

Todd Boyd, a professor of critical studies at the University of Southern California, says rap can bring races together: "It's a little more difficult to go out and talk about hate when your music collection is full of black artists. That is not to say that buying an OutKast record is the same as dealing with real people, but it is reason to hope." Ice Cube is a bit more cynical: "It's kinda like being at the zoo. You can look into that world, but you don't have to touch it. It's safe."

Nonblack performers are increasingly drawing from rap. Beck expertly combined folk and hip-hop. Hanson's hit "MMMBop" included deejay scratching. Portishead refashioned hip-hop into ethereal trip-hop. Singer Beth Orton, whose enchantingly moody album *Central Reservation* [came] out in March [1999], blends folksy guitars with samples and beats. Doug Century, author of *Street Kingdom: Five Years Inside the Franklin Avenue Posse*, studied hip-hop culture as he documented the lives of gang members; he predicts white acts will eventually dominate rap, just as white rockers pushed out rock's black forerunners. "It's possible that in 15 years all hip-hop will be white," Century says. "[Then] black youth culture will transform itself again."

Hip Hop Is the Most Important Youth Culture on the Planet

Kevin Powell, interview by Tony Karon

Kevin Powell, a writer and former senior editor for *VIBE* magazine, curated the 1999 retrospective "Hip-Hop Nation," a traveling museum exhibition of the many artifacts that attest to the history and influence of rap and hip hop on American culture during the late twentieth century.

TIME: A MAJOR MUSEUM EXPLORATION OF HIP-HOP acknowledges its rightful place in the annals of American popular culture. But doesn't putting something in a museum also imply that it's dead?

KEVIN POWELL: No, putting something in a museum does not imply that it is dead. It implies that it is important, crucial, an important part of the human journey. The art of [1980s graffiti superstar Jean-Michel] Basquiat is not dead, although he has been dead for 13 years. The art of [African American painters Romare] Bearden, [Jacob] Lawrence and others is full of life because art is about life, not death. And hip-hop is urban folk art, period. And that urban folk art is about the lives of a very unique group of people, of how they made something out of nothing, and how that nothing has come to define an entire era in many ways, be it our language, our fashion, our attitudes, our art, the way we make music, and the way we do and do not

■

Excerpted from "Hip Hop Is the Most Important Youth Culture on the Planet," by Tony Karon, www.time.com, September 22, 2000. Copyright © 2000 by Time, Inc. Reprinted with permission.

communicate across race, gender, geography, and cultures.

I think the fact that the Rock and Roll Hall of Fame (the originators of this exhibition) and now the Brooklyn Museum of Art have taken on "Hip-Hop Nation" is a mainstream institutional recognition that hip-hop is the most important youth culture on the planet, bar none. And that has been the case for some time.

Hip-hop's influence over the wider American youth culture is quite without precedent. How did it achieve this tremendous crossover appeal?

Viewed in the context of Black music in America over the past century, there's nothing surprising about hip-hop "crossing over." Blues and jazz crossed over in the 1920s, when whites rushed to Harlem to hear the music. In the 1930s, jazz became—for whites—"swing." When Black [jazz] musicians created something called bebop (a clear antecedent for hip-hop) in the 1940s, that too crossed over as whites gravitated toward the language, fashion, attitude and music of hip cats like Dizzy Gillespie and Charlie Parker. And I think most people today are clear that it was artists like Louis Jordan and Big Mama Thornton, not Elvis Presley, who created rock and roll and laid the musical foundation that crossed it over to young white people.

You can't talk about American music without talking about Black people and Black musical forms. And you cannot discuss Black music without taking in account its edginess (think of bluesman Robert Johnson, bebop innovator Charlie Parker, rocker Little Richard, soulman Otis Redding, et al.), its rebelliousness (anyone from Big Mama Thornton to Jimi Hendrix) and the fact that edginess and rebelliousness ultimately appeals to white young people as much as it does to Black young people. That and "white music" suffering slumps from time to time made the white embrace of hip-hop inevitable—has there really been anything interesting happening in rock music since the heyday of Nirvana? Not really.

Of course, this crossover success and hip-hop's current dominance of youth culture has not come without a price. What was the effect on hip-hop of its success?

Same thing that has happened to everything else black folks have done creatively: white folks control it and own it and we remain, for the most part, economic slaves. Pretty basic. And we become slaves to what the "market" tells us we should be buying. And the question I always ask young people when I speak at colleges, community centers, prisons, or wherever: What other people on the planet are allowed (and encouraged from what I have seen through my many years in and around the music industry) to call themselves the equivalent of "niggas" and "bitches" on CD and that is distributed for mass consumption?

Is hip-hop the same thing now as 25 years ago, or has it transmuted into something quite different? How have the constitution and the borders of the "hip-hop nation" changed?

Nothing stays the same. Remember, hip-hop was born on the heels of the Civil Rights Movement, a serious fiscal crisis in New York City and other urban areas, gang activity, etc. Since then we have been through the horrific Reagan era, the invasion of crack, guns, AIDS and an alleged economic boom in the 1990s—"alleged" because not too many Black people I know, even the ones with college degrees, are anything more than a paycheck away from poverty. Hip-hop has documented all of this, and more. As [poet, critic, and activist] Amiri Baraka (né LeRoi Jones) stated in "Blues People" (perhaps the most important book on Black music ever written), you can always tell where a people are at by the music they make. That means if you listen to Marvin Gaye's "What's Going On?" or Bob Marley's "Redemption Song" or Fela Kuti's "B.B.C.: Big Blind Country" you can gather what is going on with Black people at various times and in various parts of the world. Hip-hop is no different. It has evolved with the times. Now whether or not that evolution has been progressive or regressive is another discussion entirely.

Your exhibition defines the mid-'80s to 1990 as hip-hop's "Golden Years." What happened after 1990?

"The Golden Years," to me, simply means that was a period when hip-hop or, specifically, rap music, was incredibly exciting, fresh, def and diverse. There was no such thing as positive rap or negative rap, or so-called gangsta rap. Rap was rap: rhythmic American poetry, period. There has not been a time since when an N.W.A. was as popular as a Public Enemy, or where the storytelling of a Slick Rick could fall alongside the pimp strolls of a Too Short, or Roxanne Shanté was just as necessary as a Salt 'N Pepa or Queen Latifah. A lot of us cats who have lived through most or all of the history of hip-hop are the ones who proclaim that period the golden era. Why, because we can. And because we know what we are talking about. It has nothing to do with nostalgia. It has everything to do with consistently good music. Back then I used to get excited whenever a new release was coming. This year [2000] I can only count on one hand the number of hip-hop albums I have been eager to hear (Nelly, Eminem and Outkast). The corporate takeover of hip-hop has taken away much of the creativity and genius, except for the underground stuff, and that rare album where an artist is allowed to grow and shine rather than being forced to follow a formula.

Public Enemy proclaimed hip-hop the "Black CNN," and even original gangsta rappers N.W.A. said "it's not about a salary it's all about reality. . . . " Does this still hold true? What's happened to the "bearing witness" side of hip-hop? And how do the more mainstream artists view those like Mos Def, Common, the Roots, KRS One, Black Eyed Peas etc.—the acts that arise in every generation who rededicate themselves to the core values of the socially conscious rappers of the early years—are they the conscience of the hip-hop nation?

One thing [twentieth-century British essayist and novelist] George Orwell said that I very much agree with is that everything is political, which means, to me, that Nelly or Master P is as political as a Chuck D or Common. What is missing from a Nelly or Master P is a political consciousness that would force them to question WHY they have chosen a certain path and why materialism and hedonism is more important than the conditions of their communities.

That said, hip-hop has always been Black America's CNN. That has never changed. CNN shows all kinds of news, not just "positive" stuff, and that is the same for hip-hop. And hip-hop has never stopped bearing witness. Listen, for example, to Nelly's album very closely. I have been to St. Louis several times, but his album gives the close listener, via the lyrics and the accents and the attitudes, an inside look at Black working-class St. Louis. If that is not bearing witness, I don't know what bearing witness is. A lot of people, unfortunately, expect hip-hop to be overtly political. Well, we live in apolitical times and the art created in America, by and large, reflect the times. Again, how could anyone say something "positive" if there is no consciousness (or consciousness movement, for that matter) there to provide another way to look at and absorb the world.

Also, hip-hop, in spite of being a billion-dollar business, is still the blues of the working poor. And I can say this because this is the world I come from; the working poor are just basically trying to survive from day to day. I find it very classist for people to raise the issue about positive versus negative hip-hop because the same people who raise that issue don't usually discuss the death-baiting conditions which most hip-hoppers come out of. And most cats who raise that issue don't really have much to do with the hip-hop heads they are criticizing. For example, not only am I curating this exhibit, lecturing around the country, writing books, articles, etc., I now manage a young hip-hop DJ and four young hip-hop producers because I felt it important to engage people directly rather than be an armchair critic who ain't even trying to turn this apolitical madness around. It is SAFE, to me, to cling to Common (my homeboy), Mos Def (another one of my homeboys) and the other so-called socially conscious rappers. That is what the bohemians here in my Fort Greene neighborhood LOVE to do. But I RARELY see these same hip-hop bohemians in downtown Brooklyn shopping on Fulton Street on a Saturday, and I definitely don't see them walking past the Fort Greene projects on Myrtle Avenue. Which says to me there is a fear and a hatred of the working poor and their expressions. The irony of that is that cats like Common and Mos Def embrace the working poor but a lot of their fans do NOT.

My basic point: It is real easy to divide hip-hop into camps. The real challenge is to understand WHY hip-hop has deteriorated from the golden era into what we have now, and how corporate interests have played a role in that and how even the socially conscious among us are guilty of perpetuating ignorance rather than education and self-love, especially among those who need it most: Black and Latino young people.

The exhibition traces hip-hop's roots to the Bronx in the '70s. But what about the Jamaican "sound system" tradition which predated those Bronx block parties, and were clearly a major influence?

Hip-hop's roots are not Jamaican, nor Puerto Rican, nor

African American, but African. It's part of the continuum of African art forms—in some traditional African societies, for example, we find the "griot," who is the storyteller or oral historian. How is that much different from an MC telling a story (think of Slick Rick, Ice Cube, or Snoop Dogg) or rhyming about the past?

Hip-hop is a collision between African American, West Indian and Puerto Rican cultures, with the understanding that we are all African people. My point is that no matter where we were enslaved in the Western Hemisphere, be it Jamaica, Brazil or South Carolina, we as Black people held on to modes of speech, dance movements, and attitudes (what some call "cool") that formed the foundation for hip-hop's emergence in an African-American context.

So the point of the exhibition is to give people an overview of hip-hop culture and history and, really, to encourage people to do their own homework. It is not going to please everyone but that is the beauty of dialogue, is it not?

EXAMINING POP CULTURE

Does Rap Glorify Sex and Violence?

2 Live Crew, Decoded

Henry Louis Gates Jr.

When a Broward County, Florida, circuit court found
rap group 2 Live Crew's raunchy 1990 album, *As
Nasty as They Wanna Be*, to be obscene, the decision
was not only rap's biggest legal challenge yet, but it
also marked the first time any musical recording had
been judged in violation of decency standards. 2 Live
Crew and its outspoken leader, Luther "Luke"
Campbell, were acquitted of obscenity charges in
1990, but the case was widely debated throughout
American media and in academic circles alike. In this
piece, Henry Louis Gates Jr., a W.E.B. Du Bois Professor of the Humanities, the chair of Afro-American
Studies, and the director of the W.E.B. Du Bois In-
stitute for Afro-American Research at Harvard University, connects 2 Live Crew's lyrics to a rich African
American cultural heritage and argues that *As Nasty
as They Wanna Be* is valid and defensible free speech.

FOR CENTURIES AFRICAN AMERICANS HAVE BEEN
forced to develop coded ways of communicating to protect
them from danger. Allegories and double meanings, words re-
defined to mean their opposites (*bad* meaning "good," for instance), even neologisms (*bodacious*) have enabled blacks to
share messages only the initiated understood.

Many blacks were amused by the transcripts of [former
mayor of Washington, D.C.] Marion Barry's sting operation,
which reveal that he used the traditional black expression

■

Excerpted from *Rap on Rap: Straight-Up Talk on Hip-Hop Culture*, by Henry Louis
Gates Jr. (New York: Delta, 1995). Copyright © 1995 by Adam Sexton. Reprinted by
permission of the publisher.

about one's "nose being opened." This referred to a love affair and not, as Mr. Barry's prosecutors have suggested, to the inhalation of drugs. Understanding this phrase could very well spell the difference (for the mayor) between prison and freedom. 2 Live Crew is engaged in heavy-handed parody, turning the stereotypes of black and white American culture on their heads. These young artists are acting out, to lively dance music, a parodic exaggeration of the age-old stereotypes of the oversexed black female and male. Their exuberant use of hyperbole (phantasmagoric sexual organs, for example) undermines—for anyone fluent in black cultural codes—a too literal-minded hearing of the lyrics.

This is the street tradition called "signifying" or "playing the dozens," which has generally been risqué, and where the best signifier or "rapper" is the one who invents the most extravagant images, the biggest lies, as the culture says. . . . In the face of racist stereotypes about black sexuality, you can do one of two things: you can disavow them or explode them with exaggeration. 2 Live Crew, like many "hip-hop" groups, is engaged in sexual carnivalesque. Parody reigns supreme, from a takeoff of standard blues to a spoof of the black power movement; their off-color nursery rhymes are part of a venerable Western tradition. The group even satirizes the culture of commerce when it appropriates popular advertising slogans ("Tastes great!" "Less filling!") and puts them in a bawdy context. 2 Live Crew must be interpreted within the context of black culture generally and of signifying specifically. Their novelty, and that of other adventuresome rap groups, is that their defiant rejection of euphemism now voices for the mainstream what before existed largely in the "race record" market—where the records of [comedians] Redd Foxx and Rudy Ray Moore once were forced to reside.

Rock songs have always been about sex but have used elaborate subterfuges to convey that fact. 2 Live Crew uses Anglo-Saxon words and is self-conscious about it: a parody of a white voice in one song refers to "private personal parts," as a coy counterpart to the group's bluntness.

Much more troubling than its so-called obscenity is the group's overt sexism. Their sexism is so flagrant, however, that it almost cancels itself out in a hyperbolic war between the

Today They're Trying to Censor Rap, Tomorrow . . .

The First Amendment states that "Congress shall make no law . . . abridging the freedom of speech. . . ." This same clause has been incorporated into the Fourteenth Amendment so that the very same restrictions apply to the states as well.

In other words, the government has no power to restrict expression because of its message, its ideas, its subject matter, or its content. So what's the problem? I write a few songs that are purely for adult entertainment and the whole world is after me. . . .

I hope that these people who are pointing fingers are really standing up for the First Amendment and are not using the American flag to hide behind racist motives. . . .

Our environment is slowly being pulled apart, and we put people in jail for a bunch of words. Kids can't read or write, but that's not enough. We don't want them to think for themselves either. Sometimes I wonder what the starving people in Ethiopia would think about the money we've wasted on taking this to court.

Luther Campbell, "Today They're Trying to Censor Rap, Tomorrow . . . ," *Rap on Rap: Straight-Up Talk on Hip-Hop Culture*, ed. Adam Sexton. New York: Delta, 1995.

sexes. In this it recalls the intersexual jousting in Zora Neale Hurston's novels. Still, many of us look toward the emergence of more female rappers to redress sexual stereotypes. And we must not allow ourselves to sentimentalize street culture: the appreciation of verbal virtuosity does not lessen one's obligation to critique bigotry in all of its pernicious forms.

Is 2 Live Crew more "obscene" than, say, the comic Andrew Dice Clay? Clearly, this rap group is seen as more threatening than others that are just as sexually explicit. Can this be completely unrelated to the specter of the young black male as a figure of sexual and social disruption, the very stereotypes 2 Live Crew seems determined to undermine?

This question—and the very large question of obscenity and the First Amendment—cannot even be addressed until those who would answer them become literate in the vernacular traditions of African Americans. To do less is to censor through the equivalent of intellectual prior restraint—and censorship is to art what lynching is to justice.

Fighting Words: Racism, Sexism, and Homophobia in Pop and Rap

Juan Williams

Juan Williams, a staff writer for the *Washington Post*, argues in this early critique of gangsta rap that the music's roots in real inequalities do not excuse violent or hateful language directed at other historically oppressed groups.

THE RAP GROUP NWA ("NIGGERS WITH ATTI-tude") sings happily "[Expletive] Tha Police." In their hip-hop rhythms they tell listeners that "takin' out a police will make my day," and advise fans to "beat a police outta shape."

Another rap group, Public Enemy, struts on stage with a security force in paramilitary garb. A group member, Professor Griff, told reporters that Jews are responsible for "the majority of wickedness that goes on across the globe." Public Enemy also sings to its young, mostly black listeners that antisemitic black Muslim minister Louis "Farrakhan's a prophet and I think you ought to listen to what he can say to you, what you ought to do."

Ice-T, another rapper, regularly refers to women as "bitches," and makes it plain that women are treacherous, greedy, animalistic and best when disciplined by sexual abuse. Public Enemy sings a hateful song in the same vein about a woman whom they call the "Ho," and rap with righteous vin-

■

Excerpted from "Fighting Words: Speaking Out Against Racism, Sexism, and Gay-Bashing in Pop," by Juan Williams, *Washington Post*, October 15, 1989, Copyright © 1989 by Washington Post Writers Group. Reprinted with permission.

dication about how the woman took money from a man and he then "beat the bitch down till she almost died."

Heavy D and the Boyz, another rap group, have a No. 1 album, "Big Tyme," on which they tell listeners they can be "happy as a faggot in jail."

From the white racist side of the fence comes the heavy metal group Guns N' Roses with these lyrics:

"Immigrants and faggots/ They make no sense to me/ They come to our country/ And think they'll do as they please/ Like start some mini-Iran/ Or spread some [expletive] disease." Lead singer Axl Rose also sings about "niggers," whom he wants to "get outta my way/ Don't need to buy none/ Of your gold chains today."

The record industry's profitable, public venting of racism, homophobia and woman-hating in the popular music of hip, young Americans has yet to prompt any major outcry from adults, feminist groups, black civil rights groups or gay groups. Most of the parent groups concerned with lyrics in popular music confine themselves to objecting to sexual imagery that might encourage promiscuity. When it comes to racism, sexism and gay-bashing, however, there is a roaring silence.

The only public response in the black community has been the refusal of many black-oriented radio stations to play racist rap songs. Public Enemy, not content with having silenced any active criticism in the black community, goes so far as to even challenge the black radio stations for their quiet refusal to be in complicity with racism: "Radio stations I question their blackness/ They call themselves black but we'll see if they play this," sings Public Enemy.

Many white, heavy metal radio stations do not share the same moral distaste for Guns N' Roses' hateful song, and like snickering children beep out the offending words in the group's racist tirade as their knowing audiences wink.

On neither black nor white radio stations is there a straightforward response to these bigoted diatribes. There is only avoidance or silence.

The main reason for the failure to respond is fear of being accused of censorship. Jewish groups, for example, complained about Professor Griff and his antisemitic rhetoric. But they carefully avoided a scatter-gun condemnation of racism and sexist attitudes in the group's lyrics that might have weakened the focus on antisemitism and opened them to charges of censorship.

The FBI, similarly, responded to its particular concern with NWA by writing a letter to the group's record company, Priority Records, complaining that "[Expletive] Tha Police" is a song that "encourages violence against and disrespect for the law enforcement officer. . . . Advocating violence and assault is wrong and we in the law enforcement community take exception to such action." Like the Jewish groups, the FBI tried to avoid charges of censorship by limiting its concern to the song directed at police officers.

The narrowly focused criticism from both Jewish groups and the FBI was quickly dismissed among some black rappers. In a June news conference, Chuck D of Public Enemy excused the antisemitism of Professor Griff's comments by explaining the group is "not anti-Jewish, anti-anyone—we are pro-black."

This failed logic, which equates pro-black stance with bigotry toward whites and particularly Jews, has been allowed to flourish by the absence of outcry from black civil rights groups. Similarly, gay groups and groups representing black women and feminists have failed to join the dialogue and remove the rappers' transparent attempt to legitimize their bigotry, woman-hating and support of violence as progressive black thinking. . . .

The same mindset of labeling everyone who objects to racism a censor was evident in a *Rolling Stone* interview with Axl Rose. He complained about critics who object to his use of the term "nigger," by asking, "Why can black people go up to each other and say 'nigger' but when a white guy does it all of a sudden it's a big put-down? I use the word 'nigger' to describe somebody that is basically a pain in your life. . . . 'Nigger' doesn't necessarily mean black."

Aside from his stunning ignorance of American history, which gives the word 'nigger' a deadly weight that Rose apparently is unfamiliar with, the singer is on the right track. He does connect directly with an existing river of resentment among young white men against blacks and women because of preferences for blacks and women in college admissions and scholarships and the fear that competition from minorities and women may limit their chances in the job market. But when

Rose justifies his use of "nigger" as a neutral term that does not "necessarily mean black," he is either a straight-out liar or practicing historical revisionism at its most outlandish.

As Rose connects with white male resentment, NWA connects with the romance black middle-class teens have with the image of the ghetto—angry and confrontational poor black street-thugs and the glitzy cars and women of the drug dealer culture. Glazed over that teen fantasy is a generalized anger at whites as the "establishment," reflected in Public Enemy's song "Fight the Power."

NWA singer Ice Cube calls his song about killing policemen a "revenge fantasy." In the video for "[Expletive] Tha Police," NWA shows police brutally rounding up black teenagers just because they were wearing heavy gold chains and beepers. And the *Village Voice* notes that 339 Americans were shot by police officers in 1988, as if to justify NWA's exhortation to kill policemen. The paper does not cite the 151 deaths of policemen protecting the public last year. Neither does the paper cite the high rate of criminal activity among young black males nor mention the skyrocketing rate of black male murder of other black males.

But ignoring all those complex factors, the *Village Voice* seems happy to support NWA's endorsement of murder as an appropriate response to problems between police and black youth. Apparently social activism, politics and other civilized tactics are not acceptable ways for dealing with police brutality.

The strongest thread binding Guns N' Roses' racism and the racism of black rappers is a shared conceit that they are revealing the Truth.

This is where the national silence or lack of response to these simple-minded polemics becomes an abdication of responsibility in a free society. There is no other side in this argument. No one is talking to Guns N' Roses' fans about the horrors racism has inflicted on black Americans and the damage it has done to the entire society; there is no argument being heard with Public Enemy's antisemitism, no explanation of the horrors perpetrated against Jews by antisemites. There is no explanation to Ice-T's young fans of the importance of respectful male-female relationships to the creation of strong black families.

Instead there is a silence enforced by a fear of being labeled censors. The real censors today have become the young bigot, strutting on stage and defending bigotry as truth. Their defense sounds comparable to [Adolf] Hitler's defense of Nazi ideology as based on the truth of Aryan supremacy.

It is a national disgrace that in 1989 no one is standing up to a bunch of singing, young, multimillionaire bigots.

Hate, Rape, and Rap

Tipper Gore

Tipper Gore is the wife of former U.S. vice president Albert Gore Jr. and the cofounder the Parents Music Resource Center. In order to increase parental awareness of the nature of the music purchased by and for their children, the center pressured the music industry to provide parental advisory stickers on any music deemed to have explicit lyrics. In this essay, Gore speaks out against what she perceives as the denigrating content of rap lyrics and how such material has a detrimental effect on the predominantly young consumers of contemporary music.

WORDS LIKE "BITCH" AND "NIGGER" ARE DANgerous. Racial and sexual epithets, whether screamed across a street or camouflaged by the rhythms of a song, turn people into objects less than human—easier to degrade, easier to violate, easier to destroy. These words and epithets are becoming an accepted part of our lexicon. What's disturbing is that they are being endorsed by some of the very people they diminish, and our children are being sold a social dictionary that says racism, sexism, and antisemitism are okay.

As someone who strongly supports the First Amendment, I respect the freedom of every individual to label another as he likes. But speaking out against racism isn't endorsing censorship. No one should silently tolerate racism or sexism or antisemitism, or condone those who turn discrimination into a multimillion-dollar business justified because it's "real." [On

■

Excerpted from "Hate, Rape, and Rap," by Tipper Gore, *Washington Post*, January 8, 1990. Copyright © 1990 by Tipper Gore. Reprinted with permission.

an episode of the *Oprah Winfrey Show,*] television viewers saw a confrontation of depressing proportions. . . . It was one I witnessed firsthand; I was there in the middle of it. Viewers heard some black American women say they didn't mind being called "bitches" and they weren't offended by the popular rap music artist Ice-T when he sang about "Evil E" who "f—ed the bitch with a flashlight/pulled it out, left the batteries in/so he could get a charge when he begins." There is more, and worse.

Ice-T, who was also on the show, said the song came from the heart and reflected his experiences. He said he doesn't mind other groups using the word "nigger" in their lyrics. That's how he described himself, he said. Some in the audience questioned why we couldn't see the humor in such a song.

Will our kids get the joke? Do we want them describing themselves or each other as "niggers"? Do we want our daughters to think of themselves as "bitches" to be abused? Do we want our sons to measure success in gold guns hanging from thick neck chains? The women in the audience may understand the slang; Ice-T can try to justify it. But can our children?

One woman in the audience challenged Ice-T. She told him his song about the flashlight was about as funny as a song about lynching black men.

The difference is that sexism and violence against women are accepted as almost an institutionalized part of our entertainment. Racism is not—or at least, it hasn't been until recently. The fact is, neither racism, sexism nor antisemitism should be accepted.

Yet they are, and in some instances that acceptance has reached startling proportions. The racism expressed in the song "One In A Million" by Guns N' Roses, sparked nationwide discussion and disgust. But, an earlier album, that featured a rape victim in the artwork and lyrics violently degrading to women, created barely a whisper of protest. More than 9 million copies were sold, and it was played across the radio band. This is only one example where hundreds exist.

Rabbi Abraham Cooper of the Simon Wiesenthal Center, who also appeared on the *Oprah Show,* voiced his concerns about the antisemitic statements made by Professor Griff, a nonsinging member of the rap group Public Enemy; statements that gain added weight from the group's celebrity. "Jews

The Voice of Social Responsibility

Pardon the pun, but rap music is getting a bum rap. The swaggering, street-spawned sound has become even more controversial in recent months than that old adult target heavy metal, which was accused of promoting everything from Satanism to drugs.

It has been suggested that the lyrics of many rap hits, and/or the aggressive behavior of many rap groups—from Run-D.M.C. to the Beastie Boys—encourage violence, drug abuse and sexual promiscuity.

While rap does have some rough edges, the majority of rap performers actively promote social responsibility. Though rap is associated with ghetto life, many of the genre's stars are intelligent, middle-class and politically aware. They see their music as an effective means of influencing young people.

Wendy Blatt, "Rap—Voice of Social Responsibility," *Los Angeles Times*, July 19, 1987.

are wicked," Professor Griff said in an interview with *The Washington Times*. ". . . [Responsible for] a majority of wickedness that goes on across the globe."

The Simon Wiesenthal Center placed a full-page ad in *Daily Variety* calling for self-restraint from the music industry, a move that prompted hundreds of calls to the center. Yet Rabbi Cooper's concerns barely elicited a response from Oprah Winfrey's audience.

Alvin Poussaint, a Harvard psychiatrist who is black, believes that the widespread acceptance of such degrading and denigrating images may reflect low self-esteem among black men in today's society. There are few positive black male role models for young children, and such messages from existing role models are damaging. Ice-T defends his reality: "I grew up in the streets—I'm no [television personality] Bryant Gumbel."

He accuses his critics of fearing that reality, and says the fear comes from an ignorance of the triumph of the street ethic.

A valid point, perhaps. But it is not the messenger that is so frightening, it is the perpetuation—almost glorification—of the cruel and violent reality of his "streets."

A young black mother in the front row rose to defend Ice-T. Her son, she said, was an A student who listened to Ice-T. In her opinion, as long as Ice-T made a profit, it didn't matter what he sang.

Cultural economics were a poor excuse for the South's continuation of slavery. Ice-T's financial success cannot excuse the vileness of his message. What does it mean when performers such as Ice-T, Axl Rose of Guns N' Roses and others can enrich themselves with racist and misogynist diatribes and defend it because it sells? [Adolf] Hitler's antisemitism sold in Nazi Germany. That didn't make it right.

In America, a woman is raped once every six minutes. A majority of children surveyed by a Rhode Island Rape Crisis Center thought rape was acceptable. In New York City, rape arrests of 13-year-old boys have increased 200 percent [between 1988 and 1990]. Children 18 and younger now are responsible for 70 percent of the hate crime committed in the United States. No one is saying this happens solely because of rap or rock music, but certainly kids are influenced by the glorification of violence.

Children must be taught to hate. They are not born with ideas of bigotry—they learn from what they see in the world around them. If their reality consists of a street ethic that promotes and glorifies violence against women or discrimination against minorities—not only in everyday life, but in their entertainment—then ideas of bigotry and violence will flourish.

We must raise our voices in protest and put pressure on those who not only reflect this hatred but also package, polish, promote and market it; those who would make words like "nigger" acceptable. Let's place a higher value on our children than on our profits and embark on a remedial civil rights course for children who are being taught to hate and a remedial nonviolence course for children who are being taught to destroy. Let's send the message loud and clear through our homes, our streets and our schools, as well as our art and our culture.

A Culture of Violence: Gangsta Rap in Context

Robin D.G. Kelley

In the context of the 1992 Los Angeles riots (following the acquittal of the police officers involved in the March 3, 1991, beating of Rodney King), Robin D.G. Kelley finds that gangsta rap is a necessary and inevitable (if also often flawed) response to continued racial inequities in America's urban centers. The Los Angeles riots were not the first time that racial tensions had erupted in America's cities, and Kelley, a professor of history and Africana studies at New York University, traces gangsta rap's development as an expression of resistance to the economic and racial inequality that brought high unemployment, epidemic drug use, and gang violence to Los Angeles during the last third of the twentieth century.

I BEGAN WORKING ON THIS ESSAY WELL OVER A year before the Los Angeles rebellion of 1992, and at least two or three months before Rodney King was turned into a martyr by several police officers and a video camera owned by George Holliday. In fact, I had finished the essay and was about to send it out for comments when several thousand people seized the streets on May Day eve, in part to protest the acquittal of the four officers who brutally beat King thirteen months earlier [on March 3, 1991]. Of course, the rebellion enriched and complicated my efforts to make sense of

■

Excerpted from "Kickin' Reality, Kickin' Ballistics: Gangsta Rap and Postindustrial Los Angeles," by Robin D.G. Kelley, *Droppin' Science: Critical Essays on Rap Music and Hip Hop Culture*, edited by William Eric Perkins (Philadelphia: Temple University Press, 1996). Copyright © 1996 by Temple University Press. Reprinted with permission.

gangsta rap in late-twentieth-century Los Angeles, but I did not have to substantially change my original arguments. This particular genre of hip hop was, in some ways, an omen of the insurrection. The two years of "research" I had spent rocking, bopping, and wincing to gangsta narratives of everyday life were (if I may sample [critic] Mike Davis) very much like "excavating the future in Los Angeles."

Ice-T, truly the OG (original gangster) of L.A. gangsta rap, summed it up best in a 1992 *Rolling Stone* interview: "When rap came out of L.A., what you heard initially was my voice yelling about South Central. People thought, 'That shit's crazy,' and ignored it. Then NWA came and yelled, Ice Cube yelled about it. People said, 'Oh, that's just kids making a buck.' They didn't realize how many niggas with attitude there are out on the street. Now you see them."

Although the mainstream media believes it all began with the beating of Rodney King neither the hip hop community nor residents of South Central Los Angeles were surprised by that event. . . .

The L.A. rebellion merely underscores the fact that a good deal of gangsta rap is (aside from often very funky jeep music) a window into, and critique of, the criminalization of black youth. Of course, this is not unique to gangsta rap: all kinds of b-boys and b-girls—rappers, graffiti artists, breakdancers— have been dealing with and challenging police repression, the media's criminalization of inner-city youths, and the "just us" system from the get-go. Like the economy and the city itself, the criminal-justice system changed just when hip hop was born. Prisons are not designed to discipline but to corral bodies labeled menaces to society; policing is not designed to stop or reduce crime in inner-city communities but to manage it. Moreover, economic restructuring resulting in massive unemployment *has* created criminals out of black youth, which is what gangsta rappers acknowledge. But rather than apologize or preach, they attempt to rationalize and explain. Most gangsta rappers write lyrics attacking law-enforcement agencies, the denial of their unfettered access to public space, and the media's complicity in making black youth out to be criminals. Yet these very stereotypes of the ghetto as "war zone" and the black youth as "criminal," as well as their (often adolescent) struggles with notions of masculinity and sexuality, also structure and constrain their efforts to create a counternarrative of life in the inner city.

Lest we get too sociological here, we must bear in mind that hip hop, irrespective of its particular flavor, is music. Few doubt it has a message, whether they interpret it as straight-up nihilism or the words of primitive rebels. Not many pay attention to rap as art—whether the rappers are mixing break beats from Funkadelic, gangsta limpin' in black hoodies, appropriating old-school "hustler's toasts," or simply trying to be funny. Although this essay admittedly emphasizes lyrics, it also tries to deal with form, style, and aesthetics. This is a lesson cultural critic Tricia Rose has been drumming into students of African American popular culture for some time. As she puts it, "Without historical contextualization, aesthetics are naturalized, and certain cultural practices are made to appear essential to a given group of people. On the other hand, without aesthetic considerations, black cultural practices are reduced to extensions of sociohistorical circumstances."

Heeding Rose's call for a complex, more historical interpretation of cultural forms that takes account of context *and* aesthetics, politics *and* pleasure, I explore the cultural politics of gangsta rap—its lyrics, music, styles, roots, contradictions, and consistencies—and the place where it seems to have maintained its deepest roots: Los Angeles and its black environs. To do this right we need a historical perspective. We need to go back . . . way back, to the days of the OGs.

OGs in Postindustrial Los Angeles: Evolution of a Style

L.A. might be the self-proclaimed home of gangsta rap, but black Angelenos didn't put the gangsta into hip hop. Gangsta lyrics and style were part of the whole hip hop scene from the very beginning. If you never hung out at the Hevalo Club on 173rd or at Cedar Park in the Bronx during the mid-1970s, just check out Charlie Ahearn's classic 1982 film *Wild Style* documenting the early graffiti and rap scene in New York. When Double Trouble steps on stage with the fly routine, they're decked out in white "pimp-style" suits, matching hats, and guns galore. Others are strapped as well, waving real guns as part of the act. The scene seems so contemporary, and yet it was shot over a decade before Onyx recorded "Throw Ya Guns in the Air." But we need to go back even further. Back before Lightnin' Rod (Jalal Uridin of the Last Poets) recorded *Hustler's Convention* in 1973; before Lloyd Price recorded "Stagger Lee" in 1958; even before Screamin' Jay Hawkins recorded his explicitly sexual comedy rap "Alligator Wine." We need to go back to the blues, to the baaadman tales of the late nineteenth century, and to the age-old tradition of "signifying" if we want to discover the roots of the gangsta aesthetic in hip hop.

Nevertheless, while gangsta rap's roots are very old, it does have an identifiable style of its own, and in some respects it is a particular product of the mid-1980s. The inspiration for the specific style we now call gangsta rap seems to have come from the Bronx-based rapper KRS One and Boogie Down Productions, who released *Criminal Minded*, and Philadelphia's Schoolly D, who made *Smoke Some Kill*. Both albums appeared in 1987, just a few months before Ice-T came out with his debut album, *Rhyme Pays*. Ice-T was not only the first West Coast gangsta-style rapper on wax, but he was himself an experienced OG whose narratives were occasionally semiautobiographical or drawn from scenes he had witnessed or heard about on the street. . . .

A distinctive West Coast style of gangsta rap, known for its rich descriptive storytelling laid over heavy funk samples from the likes of George Clinton and the whole Parliament Funkadelic family, Sly Stone, Rick James, Ohio Players, Average White Band, Cameo, Zapp, and, of course, the Godfather himself—James Brown—evolved and proliferated rapidly soon after the appearance of Ice-T and NWA. The frequent use of Parliament Funkadelic samples led one critic to dub the music "G-Funk (gangsta attitude over P-funk beats)." Within three years, dozens of Los Angeles–based groups came onto the scene, many having been produced by either Ezy-E's Ruthless Records; Ice-T and Afrika Islam's Rhyme Syndicate Productions; Ice Cube's post-NWA project, Street Knowledge Productions; and Dr. Dre's Death Row Records. The list of West Coast gangsta rappers includes Above the Law, Mob Style, Compton's Most Wanted, King Tee, the Rhyme Syndicate,

Snoop Doggy Dogg, (Lady of) Rage, Poison Clan, Capital Punishment Organization (CPO), the predominantly Samoan Boo-Yaa Tribe, the DOC, DJ Quick, AMG, Hi-C, Low Profile, Nu Niggas on the Block, South Central Cartel, Compton Cartel, 2nd II None, W.C. and the MAAD Circle, Cypress Hill, and Chicano rappers like Kid Frost and Proper Dos.

Although they have much in common with the larger hip hop community, gangsta rappers drew ire as well as praise from their colleagues. Indeed, gangsta rap has generated more debate within and without the hip hop world than any other genre. Unfortunately, much of this debate, especially in the media, has only disseminated misinformation. Thus, it's important to clarify what gangsta rap is *not*. First, gangsta rappers have never merely celebrated gang violence, nor have they favored one gang over another. Gang bangin' itself has never even been a central theme in the music. Many of the violent lyrics are not intended literally. Rather, they are boasting raps in which the imagery of gang bangin' is used metaphorically to challenge competitors on the mic—an element common to all hard-core hip hop. The mic becomes a Tech-9 or AK-47 [types of automatic weapons], imaginary drive-bys occur from the stage, flowing lyrics become hollow-point shells. Classic examples are Ice Cube's "Jackin' for Beats," a humorous song that describes sampling other artists and producers as outright armed robbery; Ice-T's "Pulse of the Rhyme" or "Grand Larceny" (which brags about stealing a show); CPO's (Capital Punishment Organization) aptly titled warning to other perpetrating rappers, "Homicide"; NWA's "Real Niggaz"; Dr. Dre's "Lyrical Gangbang"; Ice Cube's "Now I Gotta Wet'cha"; and Compton's Most Wanted's "Wanted" and "Straight Check N' Em." Sometimes, as in the case of Ice-T's "I'm Your Pusher," an antidrug song that boasts of pushing "dope beats and lyrics/ no beepers needed" gangsta-rap lyrics have been misinterpreted as advocating criminality and violence.

Lyrical Violence: Truth and Fantasy

When the imagery of crime and violence is not used metaphorically, exaggerated and invented boasts of criminal acts should be regarded as part of a larger set of signifying practices. Performances like the Rhyme Syndicate's "My Word Is

Bond" or J.D.'s storytelling between songs on Ice Cube's *AmeriKKKa's Most Wanted* are supposed to be humorous and, to a certain extent, unbelievable. Growing out of a much older set of cultural practices, these masculinist narratives are essen-

Violence in Gangsta Rap: Whose Reality?

"Straight Outta Compton," the 1988 album by N.W.A., was about as easy to ignore as a stray bullet ripping through your living room window. If nothing else, these belligerent Southern California rappers let you know that there's madness out there. . . .

Like a lot of people, I happen to like my hip-hop hard. I don't necessarily have a problem with young rappers indulging in some good ol' American macho outlaw fantasies. But I'm not convinced it's altogether harmless either.

Early one morning recently, a young black man was shot in the back in Southeast Washington, in front of the home of a friend of mine. People came out of their houses to gather around the guy on the sidewalk. The bullet had mushroomed inside him, becoming a lump under his breastbone. He was fully conscious. "I don't want to die, man. I'm scared," he said. "I can't feel my legs, man. I don't want to die."

He died a few hours later in the hospital.

The hard-core street rappers defend their violent lyrics as a reflection of "reality." But for all the gunshots they mix into their music, rappers rarely try to dramatize that reality—a young man flat on the ground, a knot of lead in his chest, pleading as death slowly takes him in.

It's easier for them to imagine themselves pulling the trigger.

David Mills, "Rap's Hostile Fringe," *Washington Post*, September 2, 1990.

tially verbal duels over who is the "baddest motherfucker around." They are not meant as literal descriptions of violence and aggression, but connote the playful use of language itself. So when J.D. boasts about how he used to "jack them mother-fuckers for them Nissan trucks," the point is less the stealing per se than the way in which he describes his bodaciousness. He would approach the driver in the drive-through line at Mc-Donald's and announce, "Nigger, get your motherfuckin' food, leave it in the car, nigger get out!" (Ironically, in their brilliant film debut *Menace II Society*, the Hughes Brothers sampled this jack story as a representation of real live crime in South Central Los Angeles.)

When gangsta rappers do write lyrics intended to convey social realism, their work loosely resembles a street ethnography of racist institutions and social practices, told more often than not in the first person. Whether gangsta rappers step into the character of a gang banger, hustler, or ordinary working person—that is, products and residents of the 'hood—they constitute an alternative voice to mainstream journalists and social scientists. In some ways, these descriptive narratives, under the guise of objective "street journalism," are no less polemical (hence political) than nineteenth-century slave narratives in defense of abolition. When Ice Cube was still with NWA, he explained, "We call ourselves underground street reporters. We just tell it how we see it, nothing more, nothing less."

Of course, their reality is hardly objective in the sense of being detached; their standpoint is that of the ghetto dweller, the criminal, the victim of police repression, the teenage father, the crack slanger, the gang banger, and the female dominator. Much like the old baaadman narratives that have played an important role in black vernacular folklore, the characters they create appear at first glance to be apolitical individuals out only for themselves; and like the protagonist in [film-maker] Melvin Van Peebles's cinematic classic *Sweet Sweet-back's Baaadass Song*, they are reluctant to trust anyone. It is hard to miss the influences of urban toasts and pimp narratives, which became popular during the late 1960s and early 1970s. In many instances the characters are almost identical, and on occasion rap artists pay tribute to toasting by lyrically sampling these early pimp narratives.

Whereas verbal skills and creativity are the main attraction for the communities that created toasting, for some outsiders—middle-class white males, for instance—gangsta rap unintentionally plays the same role as the blaxploitation [black exploitation] films of the 1970s or, for that matter, the gangster films of any generation. It attracts listeners for whom the ghetto is a place of adventure, unbridled violence, and erotic fantasy, or an imaginary alternative to suburban boredom. White music critic John Leland, who claimed that Ice Cube's political turn "killed rap music," praised NWA because it "dealt in evil as fantasy: killing cops, smoking hos, filling quiet nights with a flurry of senseless buckshot." This kind of voyeurism partly explains NWA's huge white following and why their album, *Efil4zaggin*, shot to the top of the charts as soon as it was released. As one critic put it, "NWA have more in common with a Charles Bronson movie than a PBS documentary on the plight of the inner-cities.". . .

Economic Factors

While I'm aware that some rappers are merely "studio gangstas," and that the *primary* purpose of this music is to produce "funky dope rhymes" for our listening pleasure, we cannot ignore the ties of West Coast gangsta rap to the streets of L.A.'s black working-class communities where it originated. The generation who came of age in the 1980s during the [Ronald] Reagan–[George H.W.] Bush era were products of devastating structural changes in the urban economy that date back at least to the late 1960s. While the city as a whole experienced unprecedented growth, the communities of Watts and Compton faced increased economic displacement, factory closures, and an unprecedented deepening of poverty. The uneven development of L.A.'s postindustrial economy meant an expansion of high-tech industries like Aerospace and Lockheed, and the disappearance of rubber- and steel-manufacturing firms, many of which were located in or near Compton and Watts. Deindustrialization, in other words, led to a spatial restructuring of the Los Angeles economy as high-tech firms were established in less populated regions like the Silicon Valley and Orange County. Developers and city and county government helped the process along by infusing massive capital into suburbanization while simultaneously cutting back expenditures for parks, recreation, and affordable housing in inner-city communities. Thus since 1980 economic conditions in Watts have deteriorated on a greater scale than in any other L.A. community. . . .

Crack Comes to Town

Thus, on the eve of crack cocaine's arrival on the urban landscape, the decline in opportunities and growing poverty of black youth in L.A. led to a substantial rise in property crimes committed by juveniles and young adults. Even NWA recall the precrack illicit economy in a song titled "The Dayz of Wayback" on *Efil4zaggin* (1991) in which Dr. Dre and MC Ren wax nostalgic about the early to mid-1980s, when criminal activity consisted primarily of small-time muggings and robberies. Because of its unusually high crime rate, L.A. had by that time gained the dubious distinction of having the largest urban prison population in the country. When the crack economy made its presence felt in inner-city black communities, violence intensified as various gangs and groups of peddlers battled for control over markets. Yet in spite of the violence and financial vulnerability that went along with peddling crack, for many black youngsters it was the most viable sector of the economy.

While the rise in crime and the ascendance of the crack economy might have put money into *some* people's pockets, for the majority it meant greater police repression. Watts, Compton, Northwest Pasadena, Carson, North Long Beach, and several other black working-class communities were turned into war zones during the mid to late 1980s. Police helicopters, complex electronic surveillance, even small tanks armed with battering rams became part of this increasingly militarized urban landscape. Housing projects, such as Imperial Courts, were renovated along the lines of minimum-security prisons and equipped with fortified fencing and an LAPD substation. Imperial Court residents were now required to carry identity cards, and visitors were routinely searched. Framed by the police murder of Eula Love, the rash of choke-hold killings of African Americans taken into LAPD's custody in the early 1980s, and the videotaped beating of Rodney King, the [1980s saw] rising police brutality. As popular media coverage of the inner city associated drugs and violence with black youth, young African Americans by virtue of being residents of South Central L.A. and Compton were subject to police harassment and in some cases became the source of neighborhood distrust.

Along with the social and economic disintegration of black urban life, the combination of joblessness and poverty under Reagan–Bush, the growing viability of the crack economy and other illicit forms of economic activity, and the intensification of racist police repression, the general erosion of notions of justice, law, and order have generated penetrating critiques by gangsta rappers. MC Ren, for example, blames "the people who are holding the dollars in the city" for the expansion of gang violence and crime, arguing that if black youth had decent jobs, they would not need to participate in the illicit economy. "It's their fault simply because they refused to employ black people. How would you feel if you went for job after job and each time, for no good reason, you're turned down?" Ice-T blames capitalism entirely, which he defines as much more than alienating wage labor; the marketplace itself as well as a variety of social institutions are intended to exercise social control over African Americans. "Capitalism says you must have an upper class, a middle class, and a lower class. . . . Now the only way to guarantee a lower class, is to keep y'all uneducated and as high as possible." According to Ice-T, the ghetto is, at worst, the product of deliberately oppressive policies, at best, the result of racist neglect. Nowhere is this clearer than in his song "Escape from the Killing Fields" on *OG: Original Gangsta* (1991), which uses the title of a recent film about the conflict in Cambodia as a metaphor for the warlike conditions in today's ghettos.

Rather than attempt to explain in global terms the relationship between joblessness, racism, and the rise of crime in inner-city communities, gangsta rappers construct a variety of first-person narratives to illustrate how social and economic realities in late-capitalist L.A. affect young black men. Although the use of first-person narratives is rooted in a long tradition of black aesthetic practices, the use of "I" to signify both personal and collective experiences also enables gangsta rappers to navigate a complicated course between what social scientists call "structure" and "agency." In gangsta rap there is almost always a relationship between the conditions in which characters live and the decisions they make. Some gangsta rappers—Ice Cube in particular—are especially brilliant at showing how, if I may paraphrase [nineteenth-century political economist Karl] Marx, young urban black men make their own history, but not under circumstances of their own choosing. . . .

A Genre Spent?

While I . . . contend that most of the early gangsta rappers did not set out to glamorize crime, by the summer of 1993 gangsta rap had been reduced to "nihilism for nihilism's sake." For a moment, the hardest core, most fantastic misogynist and nihilistic music outsold almost everything on the rap scene, burying the most politically correct. In some respects, this development should not be surprising. Hard-core gangsta rap has become so formulaic that capturing even a modicum of reality no longer seems to be a priority. Ironically, the massive popularity of gangsta rap coincided with a fairly substantial increase in white suburban consumers of rap. This is in spite of the post–L.A. rebellion political climate when many commentators and cultural critics had hopes for a progressive turn in ghettocentric music, and a militant backlash against gangsta rap specifically and hip hop more generally (led mainly by middle-class male spokespersons like the Reverend Calvin Butts of Abyssinian Baptist Church in New York, African American feminist groups, and some black working-class communities concerned about violence in their midst). And, as I pointed out elsewhere in this essay, some of the most vociferous critics of gangsta rap come from within the hip hop community itself. . . .

One cannot help but notice how rap music generally, and gangsta rap in particular, has become the scapegoat for some very serious problems facing urban America. Besieged communities who are truly drowning in poverty and violence, it seems, are grasping at straws. Spokespersons for these antirap movements invoke a mythic past in which middle-class values supposedly ruled. They point to a "golden age" of good behavior, when the young respected their elders, worked hard, did not live their lives for leisure, took education seriously, and respected their neighbor's property. But this has been the claim of every generation of black intellectuals and self-appointed leaders since the end of Reconstruction. The critique of the middle class that was so powerful in some glimmers of early gangsta rap is now silenced, as is the critique of what the economy has done to people. The door is open wider than ever to more all-male schools, heavier discipline, more policing, censorship, dress codes—what amounts to an all-out war on African American youth. On the other hand, the money is still flowing for gangsta rappers, many of whom now live in the hills overlooking the ghetto. The tragedy of all this is that the gangsta rappers have gotten harder and harder, kicking more ballistics than "reality"; critics and opponents have become harder and more sweeping in their criticism, dismissing not only the gangsta stuff but the entire body of rap; and the very conditions they are concerned about remain the same.

Gangsta rap might be on its last legs, a completely spent genre that now exists in a cul-de-sac of posturing, adolescent misogyny and blood-and-guts narratives. But it would be a mistake to dismiss gangsta rap and other genres of hip hop as useless creations of the marketplace. If we want to know the political climate among urban youth, we still should listen to the music and, most importantly, to the young people who fill the deadened, congested spaces of the city with these sonic forces. And as we all probably realize, the world from which this music emerged, and to which it partially speaks, inevitably faces the further deterioration of already unlivable neighborhoods, more street crime, and increased police repression. To take their voices seriously, however, is not to suggest that they are progressive or correct, or that every word, gesture, or beat is dripping with social significance. More often than not, "G-boys" are simply out to get paid, making funky jeep music, practicing the ancient art of playing the dozens, trying to be funny, and giving the people what they want. And when they address the problems of inner-city communities, we have to keep in mind that their sharpest critiques of capitalist America are derived from the same social and economic contexts that led a lot of homies to distrust black women and each other. Nevertheless, if we learned anything from that fateful April 29 in Los Angeles, it is that, whether we like the message or not, we must read the graffiti on the walls and, as Ice-T puts it, "check the pulse of the rhyme flow."

Rap Teaches a Lesson

Murray Forman

In this opinion piece, Murray Forman suggests that
whether gangsta rap may be a true reflection of urban
reality or an exploitative style that encourages a culture of violence—or both—it nonetheless has a lesson
to impart about the way African Americans view the
police. Forman earned a graduate degree in media
and culture at Concordia University and is a contributor to the *Toronto Star*.

BLACK YOUTHS ARE RARELY HEARD IN OFFICIAL
discussions on the issue of police violence. They are, in many
cases, the backdrop to the issue, providing the bleeding bodies which catalyze the ensuing public response. When they
aren't the victims, they are reduced to members of the angry
mob, again simply as bodies clustered tightly together at noisy
demonstrations.

Police visits to youth clubs and schools don't even begin to
break the ice; the uniformed authority figure circulating in
controlled and formal settings only extends the distance between power and powerlessness. Operating with socially ceded
legitimacy, the police conduct their routinized activities in an
attempt to fulfill their mandate to "serve and protect."

For black youth, the question of whose interests are being
protected needs no further elaboration, for, on the surface, it
evidently excludes them. For blacks, the police duty of keeping the streets safe increasingly means being the subjects of
surveillance and the targets of curbside questioning. Clearly, if

■

From "Why Police Officers Should Listen to Rap Music," by Murray Forman, *Toronto Star*, July 16, 1990. Copyright © 1990 by Toronto Star Newspapers, Ltd. Reprinted with permission.

there is to be a dialogue between blacks and the police, some-one had better start listening to the kids.

Millions Sold

Rap music, in this context of anger and frustration, is one medium which provides a voice to black youth on their terms. At its best, rap is about youth power and the ability to make change. Consider this. Albums by rap artists Ice-T, KRS-1, N.W.A., and Public Enemy, have reached figures in the millions of units sold. Each of these artists, who represent only a segment of those recording in the genre, have at one time or other di-rectly addressed the issue of police harassment of blacks.

Now consider that these songs are a part of the cultural fabric of today's black youth, thoroughly internalized not only because they are hyped through the mechanisms of marketing but, more importantly, because they describe a recognizable reality. This isn't the crooning of the Motown era but an an-gry and aggressive documentation of daily experience.

Add to this the influence of Spike Lee's 1989 film *Do The Right Thing*, which deals with racist intolerance and the police killing of a young black man, or the ideological significance of the red, green, and gold Africa medallions sported by a large number of youths, and one begins to see the start of a cultural movement in which rap's influence is immeasurable.

Rap accents particular phenomena of growing up black in North America and serves to focus many of youths' dominant concerns. Marketing experts and cultural critics alike recog-nize that the success of *Do The Right Thing* was in part a result of the mass popularity of its theme song "Fight The Power" by Public Enemy. Rap's broad appeal has also crossed the color line, emerging in numerous songs by white musicians and as a mainstay at nightclubs and even campus fraternities.

KRS-1, with seven years of homelessness on his curricu-lum vitae, presents himself less as a posturing pop star than a role model and spokesman for black youth. Having been a guest lecturer at both Yale and Harvard universities, he wrote in a *New York Times* column:

> If more creative effort and dedication is not put toward ed-ucating the large, vital, and energetic populace that is this

city's black youth, the city may be consumed by the symptoms of racism. . . . Rap music, stigmatized by many as mindless music having no socially redeeming value, can be a means to change.

His own music bounces from the rational request for black cultural history as a part of the school curriculum in "You Must Learn to Bo! Bo! Bo!," a narrative about a violent run-in with "a redneck cop" and the "street knowledge" that informs black youths' own, often violent, responses.

For many rappers today, the message begins with a demand for cultural education programs as a precursor to equal rights and justice, ending with Malcolm X's intonement, ". . . by any means necessary." It is precisely this last sentiment that has white and black community leaders as well as police forces worried.

It is feared that youths listening to rap may fall into a rhythm of violence and intolerance, further complicating the process of negotiating an urban detente between blacks and the police. This position regards rap as an inflammatory force which simplifies the situation, breaking it down to a struggle between "us" and "them." As reflected by the braggadocio of N.W.A.'s " ———Tha Police," being "bad" is better than being smart and an Uzi solution is tantamount to an easy solution.

Anti-Drug Theme

While rap songs which veer toward vengeance undoubtedly exist, there are also many which seek to examine society's structural problems. In these songs, the emphasis on educational, anti-drug, and anti-gang themes prevail, taking a positive and rational stand on the crises facing black youth. As Ice-T, a proponent of what is known as "gangster rap," states in "You Played Yourself":

" . . . Society's fault? No! Nobody put the crack into the pipe, nobody made you smoke off your life, you thought that you could do dope and stay cool? Fool, you played yourself . . ."

In this age when so much of our social awareness is gleaned from popular culture and the media it becomes crucial that our authorities keep abreast of what is happening around them. To ignore or dismiss a growing phenomenon such as rap would be a grave error and, arguably, a failure in their ability to comprehend their role as authority.

Our police forces need to be listening to rap in all of its forms, even if it means listening to mean-spirited, foul-mouthed attacks on them. They need to learn how to read the codes of style which accompany the hip-hop scene and how to interpret the poses at street level. They need to understand the meanings of curbside vernacular and, for example, that "dope" can be a positively loaded term with no reference to drugs whatsoever.

The police don't have to like rap. They do, however, need to comprehend the messages being kicked with full force and to synthesize them, working within the contexts presented. The police are already a part of the "text," albeit often as the enemy, but still operating within the music itself in an important and meaningful way. In this regard, they had better understand where they are situated in the songs and listen closely for clues about how best to diffuse tempers before trouble starts.

If they want to repair the damage already done—if, in effect, they want to change the words to the songs—they need to put real action behind their own rhetorical rap and start listening to the voices of black youth.

Marketing Gangsta Rap: Where Is the Real Danger?

Ronin Ro

As gangsta rap surged in popularity during the 1990s, its authenticity as a form of reportage on inner-city conflict began to give way to a formula (albeit a successful one) that promoted pure fantasies of the "hard" lifestyle of guns, drugs, and crime. The line between fact and fantasy was not always clear, however, and Ro argues that the resulting gangsta fashion that came to dominate hip-hop culture for both blacks and whites has yielded negative effects. Ronin Ro is also the author of *Have Gun Will Travel: The Spectacular Rise and Violent Death of Death Row Records*.

1992: THE SKIES ARE SUNNY AND PEOPLE ARE GET-ting stabbed. Kid Frost walks through a mob of car enthusiasts who view the violence as a small annoyance. The gang scene is out of control. 'Bangers in various sets confirm that recent "riots" (said to protest the verdict in the Rodney King beating) were more gang-related than anything: some 'bangers admit that they saw the looting on TV and, bored, with nothing pressing on their schedule and in need of money, hurried to downtown's best stores before thieves stole everything.

The media pounces on the story: the right-wingers call it civil disobedience and attribute the looting to Black or Latino "criminals"; leftist magazines like *The Source* see it as political rebellion. Suddenly, dime-a-dozen gangsta rappers appear in

∎

Excerpted from *Gangsta: Merchandizing the Rhymes of Violence*, by Ronin Ro (New York: St. Martin's Press, 1996). Copyright © 1996 by Ronin Ro. Reprinted with permission.

Rolling Stone, with white writers indulging their liberalism and running half-page quotes from each. These non-skilled rappers believe their own press clippings and pat each other on the back. . . .

Before NWA's *Straight Outta Compton* album, hip-hop acts tried to steer youth in a more positive direction: Groups like Boogie Down Productions and Public Enemy told them to stop eating beef, to affect more natural hairstyles and to study their history; there were songs like "Stop the Violence," which urged kids to coexist in peace; and the hip-hop party was a unifying event filled with real MCs and not "rappers." A real MC (mic controller) says what they feel from the heart; they don't exploit sex and violence: they'll deliver good punch lines, insults, similes and metaphors. A "rapper" is an asshole who sits and concocts bull's-shit that will hit the pop chart or radio and make them rich; a "rapper" is more concerned with creating a catchy hook instead of dropping true lyrics.

Before NWA, we used to have more MCs and less rappers and all was right with the world. At these parties, white kids partied with Blacks and Latinos, straight partyers didn't bash gays, poor kids didn't rob their more affluent dance partners, urban youth didn't deride suburban, Jews didn't clash with Gentiles, and Korean grocers weren't demonized. Hip-hop was seen as a form that would inspire political change; we all believed that rap performers breaking barriers on shows like *American Bandstand* and *Soul Train*, and hearing our music in commercials for Polly-O String Cheese and Flintstones Fruity Pebbles was merely the first step to running the old folks out of office and replacing them with our political representatives, the Chuck Ds, Rakims and KRS-Ones. Rap albums were selling in the millions, MTV was kissing the rappers' asses, a worldwide audience formed and the music was filled with nothing but hope. Hip-hop would empower the inner city; we didn't see its perversion into the more "marketable" 'hood coming. We were going to be galvanized by art, not demonized.

In our own way, we were as idealistic as the hippies of the sixties, and we truly believed that everything would be all right; we would listen to our music, learn our history and unite to become a political force to be reckoned with. And we were on our way to becoming that just as NWA arrived to confirm the commercial viability of a strange new form of hip-hop.

For years, everyone credited Ice-T or KRS-One of Boogie Down Productions as the father of gangsta rap until KRS-One acceded that Schoolly D's "P.S.K." single (about Philadelphia's Park Side Killers gang) may have hit radio a second before BDP's *Criminal Minded* album. "Oh yeah, that did come first, right?" he said during a particularly grueling interview I conducted for *Spin*.

But, where Schoolly combined Run-DMC's prepackaged hardness with the explicitness of Slick Rick's "La-Di-Da-Di," KRS-One actually did produce the first true gangsta rap effort: instead of consciously fusing elements for effect, KRS' "9MM Goes Bang" touched upon events that Kris Parker actually grew up around, and it was a helluvalot more chilling.

From there, Ice-T abandoned his electropop roots and delivered his own Schoolly-like anthem, "6 in the Morning," which found an audience with those who were actually the victims of the LAPD's predawn drug raids. From there, Ice Cube wrote "Boyz-N-the 'Hood," another Schoolly-like work with Run-DMC–influenced deliveries, that recontextualized the East Coast b-boy aesthetic for West Coast gangland. Cube couldn't convincingly write about attending jams in violent New York nightspots like the Latin Quarter or Union Square or about bombing the Bronx-bound 4 train with sharp boxcutters at the ready, so he touched upon his immediate environment, the gang-plagued neighborhoods, drug-related shootouts and draconian oppressiveness of the LAPD. By addressing these themes, he made one of the most primitive and profane rap albums ever recorded stand as the perfect encapsulation of a period in L.A.'s troubled history. Most importantly they delivered a work that moved Los Angeles rap past its embarrassing embryonic phase. Before NWA, the West Coast hip-hop scene was limited to exploitative Golan Globus films *(Breakin'* or *Rappin')*, "Planet Rock" knockoffs and bizarrely coiffed King Tut wannabes.

New York had the hardest groups (LL Cool J, Run-DMC, BDP, Big Daddy Kane); the comedians (Biz Markie, UTFO, Slick Rick); the political theorists (Public Enemy and Boogie Down Productions); the lyrical virtuosos (Rakim, Kool G Rap, KRS-One, Kane and Chuck D); and the trend-setting producers (Marley Marl, DJ Mark, Scott La Rock and the Bomb Squad). But *Straight Outta Compton* changed that: "The record not only put listeners within point-blank range of LA gang mentality, but it did so nonjudgmentally, without any sense of moral distance, going so far on some tracks as to use black-on-black violence as the metaphoric base for some of the group's boasting," as *Village Voice* writer Greg Tate pointed out.

By fusing the blue comedy of Redd Foxx, Dolomite and Richard Pryor to the urban grittiness of Iceberg Slim, then injecting the social relevancy of Public Enemy and Boogie Down Productions, five bored Compton teenagers were able to go from religiously attending concerts by visiting New York groups Run-DMC and LL Cool J, to realizing their dreams of hip-hop stardom. *Straight Outta Compton* "shook the shit out of East Coast rappers and fans alike," wrote Tate, ushering in the era of gangsta rap and, most importantly, showing L.A. rappers that they too could sell a million copies to a built-in audience if they fashioned an image based upon the gang culture prevalent in California since the turn of the century. . . .

As many O.G.s (Original Gangsters who are older and survived to see this era) will point out, "gangbanging" back then meant riding the bus into someone's 'hood and mixing it up with the hands, bats, chains and maybe knives.

After 1980, however, cocaine was introduced and many gangs saw drug sales as a way of earning money; many sets (gangs) converted their neighborhoods into block-long drug spots and competition became as cutthroat as it was between stockbrokers on Wall Street. Guns were everywhere and gang members began living out Oliver Stone's screenplay for *Scarface*; the competition was murdered, Los Angeles became a war zone and the LAPD adopted fascistic methods in an effort to reduce the body count. Before NWA's *Straight Outta Compton*, however, the only examination of the culture could be found in Dennis Hopper's *Colors*, a pro-LAPD film that granted the Crips and the Bloods a national audience.

"At the beginning we point out that there are 250 men and women working in law enforcement against 600 gangs with over 70,000 members," a beleaguered Hopper told the *L.A. Times* in March of 1988, confirming that the gang problem was clearly not, as authorities in 1926 felt, something easily solved.

NWA figured that injecting gang-related topics, slang and fashions into their act would guarantee a built-in audience with the thousands of gang members infiltrating L.A., and they were right. But their album also struck a chord with white audiences bored with Run-DMC's tame heavy metal–styled anthems. With harder music and homicidal attitudes, as well as a hardcore fashion sense, which they later admitted stealing from Run-DMC, NWA upped the ante, became the band to beat and promoted the gangbanger ideology.

They were viewed as Leadbellies for a new age: they cursed and threatened anyone in their path, and they offered an alternative to merely being victimized by societal ills (as Melle Mel said he'd been, on Old School pioneer Grandmaster Flash's seminal "Message" of seven years before). Just as hip-hop's more positive acts were trying to steer the audience into nationalism, unity and political awareness, NWA's nihilism was set to more appealing music. The "positive" acts were viewed as anachronisms by a hyperprogressive audience and discarded while the one-dimensional gangstas signed six-figure album deals and dragged hip-hop away from its roots.

Gun homicide had been the leading cause of death for black teens since 1969, and while the mere presence of gangsta rap was not the sole cause of escalating murder rates, the casual attitudes that gangsta rappers exhibited while discussing Black on Black murder somehow made homicide acceptable. The music equated guns with masculinity, depicted them as "problem solvers" and stressed that, since other kids probably owned guns of their own, shouldn't we all be strapped?

Fourteen kids (age nineteen and under) will be killed in gun accidents, suicides, or homicides before sunset. (For this age group, the murder rate has increased 125 percent between 1984 and 1990.) Not even all natural diseases combined can equal the annual number of teenage deaths attributed to firearms. One out of every 28 Black males born is likely to be murdered; for whites, the ratio is one out of 164. If you're Black, the chances are higher of being murdered by one of your own: 1990 saw 93 percent of Black murder victims killed by other Blacks.

Although firearm homicide is still the number one cause of death for Black males aged fifteen to thirty-four, and the number two cause of death for all fifteen- to twenty-four-year-olds, a new handgun is still produced every twenty seconds. By the time you finish reading this paragraph, another gun will exist. Don't be fooled: death is random and senseless. There are more than two hundred million firearms in the hands of the American public (sixty-seven million of which are handguns). Those gun owners who religiously follow gangsta rap will have no compunctions about shooting. This is the only controversy surrounding gangsta rap—this, and whether these primitive rappers deserve to have record deals; because rap can be a "Black CNN" and a "voice of the disenfranchised diaspora" and all of that other shit, but first and foremost, it's a form of entertainment. If gangsta rappers have to rely on this shock-value bullshit for attention, then maybe they don't have any talent and the status of their record deals should be reevaluated.

Instead of urging listeners to "fight the power" or improve their community, as Boogie Down Productions and Public Enemy had done, gangsta rap told listeners to direct their anger against their own kind. And soon, as they had done when the nationalists topped the sales charts, the audience began to listen. Whereas P.E. and BDP helped wean youth off of the addictive habits of gold jewelry, self-hate and straightened hair, gangsta rap influenced youth to buy guns and adopt a paranoid victim's worldview.

While the mainstream media haggled over censorship issues surrounding the music, the gangsta rappers began translating their on-wax fantasies into full-scale reality. Many were soon entangled in legal problems and shootouts, and their listeners grew further entranced. Soon, the listener—young, lacking role models or authority figures, and somewhat bored with life—would accept the gangsta rapper's lyrics as gospel.

What's most shameful is the East Coast reaction to the string of platinum albums streaming from the West Coast. At first, certain East Coast artists vehemently denounced gangsta rap's regressive attitudes, and tried to counteract them with positive, socially conscious albums; but when these albums failed to match the million-plus sales of a Too $hort or a DJ Quik, they rethought their philanthropy and began injecting gangsta elements into their verse.

Another extreme East Coast reaction came from artists like

Tim Dog, who tried building careers around attacking West Coast rap with the same style and attitude. By substituting South Bronx housing projects for Compton 'hoods and describing the very same scenarios, artists like Tim hoped to garner platinum sales. The apotheosis arrived when Kool G Rap, once known for lyrical intricacy, enlisted Ice Cube's producers and simplified his style, hoping to produce a platinum-selling work, and when the group Onyx fashioned their own gangsta rap persona and tried to popularize a new subgenre called "horror-core." Horror core was to hip-hop what death metal is to Brahms or Mozart. Now the East Coast hip-hop scene is rife with death-obsessed groups like the Gravediggers or the Flat-linerz, with the drug culture chic of artists like Biggie Smalls and Fat Joe, with trigger-happy acts like Smif-N-Wessun and M.O.P. and with Snoop impersonators of every shape and size.

With New York groups incorporating gangsta elements, the West Coast continuing to generate million-dollar sales and the Midwest sounding like NWA circa 1988, the formerly marginal strains of gangsta rap, now set to ParliaFunkadeli-cized grooves [based on the 1970s groups Parliament and Funkadelic], have come to define hip-hop as a whole. And it's fast on its way to casting its shadow—projecting the artists' drug abuse, misogyny and self-hate—over this generation.

That gangsta rap has grown so large may explain why white kids now affect gangbanger fashions and attitudes in Little Rock, Arkansas; it may shed light on why murder figures are rising in low-income areas; antisociality is now the norm, and the gun, and not mediation, is the primary arbiter of social conflict.

EXAMINING POP CULTURE

Case Study in Controversy: Eminem and Gay Bashing

Eminem: Genius or Hatemonger?

Chris Norris

Perhaps no artist of the late-twentieth and early twenty-first centuries has been more controversial—or more successful—than Eminem. His horror-movie fantasies of drugs, violence, and rape, often voiced through his dark alter ego, "Slim Shady," caused a stir in 1999 with his Dr. Dre–produced *The Slim Shady LP*, but it wasn't until the release of *The Marshall Mathers LP* (2000) that Eminem became a cultural lightning rod, igniting a firestorm of debate that extended from record buyers all the way up to the 2000 presidential campaign. A white rapper who appeals to predominantly white suburban teens, Eminem has brought a particularly savage version of gangsta rap to middle America and, as a result, drawn supporters and detractors in seemingly equal numbers. Chris Norris, a contributor to *Spin* magazine, attempts to give a balanced assessment of Eminem as both a musical talent and a cultural phenomenon.

SHHH! I THINK EMINEM'S TRYING TO TELL US something.

When he began his set on the recent Anger Management tour with a *Blair Witch*–style film depicting him as a chainsaw-wielding psycho, that seemed like kind of a hint. And when he then made his entrance in a *Friday the 13th* hockey mask, that too seemed like a little insinuation there. And when, on *The Marshall Mathers LP*, the world's self-proclaimed "most meanest MC" strangled a woman, cut a guy's head off, raped his

■

Excerpted from "Lunatic Genius, Potty-Mouth, Hatemonger, or All of the Above?: Some Thoughts on the Surreal Slim Shady," by Chris Norris, www.spin.com, January 2001. Copyright © 2001 by Spin Magazine. Reprinted with permission.

mother, and Al Gore–ishly took credit for inventing violence itself—all before the end of the first verse—well, call me crazy, but that seemed like he was making a point of some kind.

But perspective gets tricky when you've had the kind of year Marshall Mathers has had [in 2000]. Within 12 months, the 27-year-old rapper known as Eminem has bashed teen-poppers and beefed with hip-hoppers; been divorced from his wife and sued by his mom; lost custody of his daughter, Hailie Jade; been arrested on assault charges (for allegedly pistol-whipping a bouncer) and weapons charges (for allegedly pulling a gun on a rival rap group); been denounced for misogyny and condemned for homophobia—and, somewhere along the way, sold 7 million records. It was an appropriately sci-fi spectacle for the Year 2000: a white MC with the fastest-selling solo album of all time. As [basketball player] Charles Barkley told a reporter, "You know it's going to hell when the best rapper out there is white and the best golfer is black."

But not even the hard-driving Tiger Woods has ruffled as many feathers as Eminem, who has been name-checked by everyone from Elton John to Boy George to the presidential hopefuls. In September 2000, Lynne Cheney [wife of Dick Cheney, George W. Bush administration vice president] went so far as to bust some Eminem lyrics in a Senate hearing. "'Wives, nuns, sluts,'" she recited. "Whoever 'the bitches' might be. He will kill them slowly, leaving enough air in their lungs so their screaming will be prolonged. He will paint the forest with their blood. 'I got the machete from O.J.,' he shouts. 'Bitch, I'm-a kill you.'"

While some wives, nuns, and sluts were doubtless disconcerted, others probably caught the deafening hyperbole in the lines, a shock-jock overkill that runs throughout Eminem's second multiplatinum LP and made many condemnations faintly ridiculous. Our old friend, the anti-rap crusader C. DeLores Tucker, even rejoined the fight, railing against the record's "advocacy of incest, sacrilege, rape, and sodomy," despite the fact that it's mostly con on the last issue (more on that later). Criticism of the record got to sound almost as crazy as the record itself. "I like how they called his style 'viloporn,'" says Eminem's A&R man, Dean Geistlinger, referring to a statement announcing Cheney's speech. "That was dope. Viloporn."

Shock as Entertainment

In fact, *The Marshall Mathers LP* does deserve a new designation—not for style, however, but for entertainment format. Though composed and performed by the hottest rapper and greatest producer in the business, it isn't simply a rap record. Functionally, it's a combination rap record, comedy album, cartoon show, and horror movie. It was made by a star whose diverse talents enable strange fluidity among genres and who has a sure knowledge of each one's rules. His multitongued pop vernacular, born and forged in hip-hop, is a big part of both Eminem's massive success and the confusion surrounding him. In a new documentary on the slasher films of the '70s, director John Landis describes the difference between watching a Hitchcock thriller and watching one of the new-jack horror films like *The Texas Chainsaw Massacre*. "When you're watching a Hitchcock movie, you are in suspense as a result of being in the hands of a master," he says. "With some of these other films, the people making them are untrustworthy. You're not in the hands of a master; you're in the hands of a maniac."

This is the effect of the storyteller Slim Shady, who raps, "I'm just as fucked-up as you woulda been if you'd-a been in my shoes" and, by most indications, is probably right. Eminem, who was born a year before *Chainsaw* was released and who name-checks it in his record's first verse, knows this narrative technique and has employed it masterfully, evading both predictability and responsibility. In the process, he has also affected the tastes and attitudes of just about every young person in the country. And this makes the outcry over Eminem something more than politics as usual.

Part of the scary brilliance of the Eminem Project is its Trojan Horse quality, the way this vile bundle of rage and dysfunction has been packaged in such shiny, non-childproof wrapping. If Mathers goes to puzzling lengths trashing boy-band singers—"I'm anti-Backstreet and Ricky Martin/With instincts to kill 'N Sync; don't get me started," etc.—part of the reason might be that, until he opens his mouth, he could pass for one himself. (Eminem nightmare #325: the October *Teen People*, which hypes its Mathers cover story next to the lines "9 New Tricks for Perfect Skin" and "Cool Looks Modeled By 98°.") Once a member of '90s hip-hop's subgenre of crazy white rappers—including RA the Rugged Man, Cage, and others—the angel-faced rapper is now slipping his Vicodin and snuff tales in between comic books and Clearasil. Buoyed by the seductive tracks of Dr. Dre, the man who brought gang signs to the strip mall, he's representing underground in the most mainstream places possible. This has puzzled people on both sides of the fence.

"When I first heard the second album, I was like, 'Why is he dissing Britney Spears?'" recalls DJ Milo Berger, of the indie hip-hop group the High & Mighty, Eminem's openers on a European tour. "But then I realized he's really living in an MTV world now. He's writing about what he's experiencing, which every good MC should."

To survive that neutralizing world, Eminem has become a self-aware cartoon, an everykid rebel like Bart Simpson or, in his own words, "a skinny, 26-year-old Cartman"—i.e., *South Park*'s famous potty-mouth. This is the flip side to Eminem's horror-film persona, realized in The Slim Shady Show, the other film feature of his Anger Management set. Quoting *South Park* and Hanna-Barbera, the short, like some of the best hip-hop, is sick, stylish, and hilarious. (The plot involves Slim's gang avenging a lost b-ball game on the *South Park* gang with a handful of Viagra tablets and an Ex-Lax bar.) But whatever format it takes, the rapper's cartooning is at least partially autobiographical. And this fundamental hip-hop conceit makes Eminem, even at his most cartoonish, resonate much differently than other two-dimensional characters.

Violence, Sexism, and Homophobia

That brings us to the tightly packed lyrics on *The Marshall Mathers LP*, which are vicious in every sense of the word. They attack enemies famous, obscure, and, in some cases, not particularly hurting for attackers. Rap's tradition of misogyny and homophobia makes lines like the now-infamous "Hate fags?/ The answer's yes" hard to shrug off, especially when their obviously intelligent author explains his generally gay-baiting use of the word "faggot" as a generic playground taunt—a distinction that seems to have eluded many of his supporters. "Eminem knows what his fans want to hear," reads one posting on the antimusic.com site. "Fags should stay away and live on a leper island." Some posters feel Eminem's pain: "I have a fag uncle. I hate my uncle, and I hate fags. . . . All [Eminem] is trying to say is he dislikes homosexuals and thinks it's not right to be gay." Another just writes to express heartfelt admiration: "I am a 17-year-old female. I really love Eminem and his music. I look up to him as a human and for his music. . . . If you have any comments please feel free to contact me. . . . You FAGGOTS WILL DIE. Thank you, Carly."

While Eminem definitely didn't invent such sentiments, he has certainly given them a coolness and presentability they didn't have a few years ago, which is a pretty shitty thing to have on your résumé. Being a hip-hop head has always meant having to say you're sorry—to Jews for liking Public Enemy; to the police for liking N.W.A; to Koreans for liking Ice Cube; to women for liking just about anybody. At this point, many fans blow off extramusical moralizing, assuming that hip-hop's streety, volatile lyricism will always defy polite society and that that's sort of the point. With Eminem, that attitude has truly gone mainstream.

"I think his success represents in a way the decline of the whole p.c. regime of the early '90s," says MTV's Kurt Loder, who has spent many hours interviewing and pondering Eminem. "People are just tired of being told what they can say, what they can listen to. Whether or not you like what he's saying, what he's saying really is him, and he's not tailoring it for any particular audience. I think the reality of it is what's so appealing. He's saying what's on his mind. And surely a lot of people are not going to like what's on his mind."

Or, goes the argument—as Eminem well knows—they'll like it all too much. During Eminem's recent concert performances of "Role Model," a screen behind the stage flashed advice like "Do What I Say," "Take Pills," and "Have Sex" over the spiraling black-and-white backdrop that '50s films used to connote hypnotic mind control. It was an arena-sized in-joke. For someone who claims not to give a fuck, Eminem is constantly rapping about his influence on others—defiantly and sarcastically, always playing with the idea of words and responsibility. "I think I was put here to annoy the world/And destroy your little four-year-old boy or girl." (Interestingly, the only word on the entire album that's actually bleeped out is a word that only became an obscenity two years ago: "Columbine"—a disaster widely blamed on pop-cultural poisoning.)

Irony or Irresponsibility?

While enjoying Eminem would seem to require getting the irony, that irony comes entwined with a lot of other very real, very volatile emotions. The *Marshall Mathers* song "Kim," for instance, is almost certainly the first song to be cited in divorce proceedings, classified as "Intentional Infliction of Emotional Distress" in his wife's suit for its depiction of "horrific domestic violence against the wife resulting in her grisly murder." The song is indeed horrific, a nightmare dramatized. On it, Eminem doesn't sound like he's battling or wisecracking, rather auditioning for an Abel Ferrara [director of *Bad Lieutenant* and *Body of Evidence*] movie. He shrieks his rhymes, reprising a rage- and grief-laden domestic dispute that's hard to imagine chuckling at or bumping along to in your ride. Both its tone and autobiographical source make "Kim" pretty clearly something other than a sick joke, and Eminem a far more slippery creature than a simple shock rapper.

For words like these, words that aren't just gags or battle rhymes, the ever-savvy author has another explanation. We are to simply blame his alter ego, Slim Shady—a personage literary critics would call, with considerable understatement, "an unreliable narrator." It's a slick trick, some would say, a morally weak dodge. But artistically, it's totally legitimate. This may be what Eminem's defensibility rests on: whether you can call someone an artist who works out his problems with the women in his life onstage with a blow-up doll.

Exactly one month before election day, America's No. 1 viloporn rapper was getting ready to rock our nation's satire capital. While his crew sampled exotic appetizers ("Yo, can I get some of that edamame flow?"), Eminem sat in his dressing room and prepared for his role in the season premiere of *Saturday Night Live*. Since the embattled rapper had instituted a complete press blackout, the world will just have to imagine the substance of his dressing-room tête-à-têtes with Farrah Fawcett and the Fonz (who came to introduce his bleach-blond teenage son, Max Winkler).

Onstage, however, Eminem presented a powerful if oblique challenge to those painting him as a simple hatemonger. In his white ball cap and baggy sweater, he stood next to the slim, blonde British singer Dido and performed the *Marshall Mathers* song "Stan," which samples Dido's acid-jazzy "Thank You." "Dear Slim," he began, "I wrote you but you still ain't callin'/I left my cell, my pager, and my home phone at the bottom." In this odd epistolary rap—told entirely in letters from an increasingly deranged fan—the song's story unfolds so smoothly and with such expert pacing that it's easy to overlook what an amazing literary and musical performance it is. Ending with a chilling murder-suicide described in a previous Eminem song, "Stan" is a sharp and chilling simulacrum that shows self-awareness without taking any blame. "I actually think that song has an incredible social conscience," Dido said later. *SNL* producer Lorne Michaels came to Mathers' dressing room to compliment him. "One thing I do know is writing," he told the rapper. "And you're a great writer.". . .

Eminem's album is, in its way, obsessed with the creation of a self. It's a dark, hateful, funny, and cruel sort of The Miseducation of Slim Shady, penned by someone who may not be a moral artist, a profound artist, or even, in the long run, a significant artist. But he's definitely one of the increasingly rare chartmongers who actually deserves the title "recording artist." *The Marshall Mathers LP* isn't just a sick joke, just a cartoon, or just a horror movie. Its lurid raps and murderous fantasies aren't all shock raps but often outpourings of angst and spite, the kind of things we comfortably called art when Kurt Cobain—another small, blond, witty, working-class former victim of bullies—set them to Beatlesque melodies rather than hyperkinetic rhyme schemes. And just because the tales aren't literal doesn't mean they're not real.

No Excuse for Eminem

Eric Boehlert

Eric Boehlert, a frequent contributor to the online journal *Salon*, takes a strongly critical stance against both the content of Eminem's *The Marshall Mathers LP* and those music and cultural critics who have refused to condemn the rapper's lyrics. According to Boehlert, not even the arguable artistic merits of *The Marshall Mathers LP*'s musical production or Eminem's verbal skill should excuse lyrics that preach hatred and violence against women and gays, nor should those journalists who support the album be excused for implicitly condoning Eminem's irresponsibility.

ACCOUNTANTS FOR INTERSCOPE RECORDS AND rapper Eminem weren't the only ones cheering last week when the star's 2000 album, "The Marshall Mathers LP," debuted at No. 1 in blockbuster style. The aggressively demented album, which features the white rapper weaving rapid-fire tales about rape, faggots, bitches, drug overdoses and throat cuttings, sold 1.7 million copies in just seven days, according to SoundScan, becoming the second-biggest-selling debut week in industry history—and certainly the most successful showing by a rapper ever.

Also applauding the sales tally for the new record were the nation's music critics, who, for the most part, have been wildly enthusiastic about the rapper's work. "Eminem has not only become the legitimate heir to Tupac Shakur and the Notorious B.I.G.," gushed *Newsweek*, "he's arguably the most com-

■

Excerpted from "Invisible Man," by Eric Boehlert, www.salon.com, June 7, 2000. Copyright © 2000 by Salon. Reprinted with permission.

pelling figure in all of pop music." Fed up with watching boy bands and girl pop posers win over the hearts of consumers, critics welcomed the chance to bond with fans of some tougher sounds. . . .

Eminem, 26, is from Detroit; he has short blond hair and an insolent stare. His rap debut came in the little-noticed form of "Infinite," which was void of Eminem's now trademark slurs. It flopped. In '97 a sample of Eminem's new, harder sound landed in the hands of Dr. Dre, a founding member of hardcore rap group NWA and mentor of Snoop Dogg. Dre signed Eminem to his Interscope-distributed label; by the time 1999's "The Slim Shady LP" was released, Eminem's single "My Name Is" was already a blockbuster in the burbs. The album went on to sell 3 million copies and remained near the top of the album charts for the better part of a year.

> Bitch I'ma kill you!
> You don't wanna fuck with me
> Girls leave—you ain't nuttin' but a slut to me
> Bitch I'ma kill you!
> . . .
> You better kill me!
> I'ma be another rapper dead for poppin' off at the mouth
>   with shit I shouldn'ta said
> But when they kill me—I'm bringin' the world with me
> Bitches too!
> You ain't nuttin' but a girl to me
> – "Kill You," a song about Eminem's mother

Of course, Eminem has the right to rap about whatever he wants, and if executives at Interscope are comfortable releasing that sort of CD, then the debate ends right there. But should the nation's tastemakers, the ones supposedly pondering the connection between art and society, align themselves with an artist as blatantly hateful, vengeful and violent as Eminem?

Not only have Eminem's foul lyrics not sparked a debate among serious music observers, they've barely even caused a stir. It'd be as if Bret Easton Ellis wrote the murderous *American Psycho* and no critic questioned his judgment or the book's content—and those who did pause briefly to consider the book's moral or social implications simply dismissed the consequences because: A) the story's only fiction and B) Ellis is a really, really good writer. That's basically what most music journalists have done as they eagerly explain away Eminem's psychopathic subject matter.

So afraid are music's defenders to give an inch in their battle with the Bill Bennett [former "drug czar" for the George H.W. Bush administration and author of *The Book of Virtues*] moralists of the world that they're now championing an artist who raps nearly nonstop on his new slanderous CD about sluts, guts, cocaine and getting "more pussy than them dyke bitches total."

Of course, the problem with "Marshall Mathers" isn't simply R-rated lyrics. They're nothing new, although Eminem has taken them to a new and oddly focused level. Other rap records might create a world of clichéd bitches and ho's to lay down party beats for good times or hold up a mirror to their environment. Some of the better ones (Jay-Z, Ice Cube, Ice-T) even took time out occasionally to reflect on the consequences of their gangsta actions. But Eminem's not interested in any of that. Instead, the rapper simply delivers 75 minutes of nearly nonstop hate (that is, when he's not whining about his fame). How hateful? According to GLAAD (the Gay and Lesbian Alliance Against Defamation), the album "contains the most blatantly offensive homophobic lyrics we have ever heard. Ever."

> New Kids on the Block, sucked a lot of dick
> Boy-girl groups make me sick
> And I can't wait 'til I catch all you faggots in public
> I'ma love it [hahaha]
>
> . . .
>
> Talkin' about I fabricated my past
> He's just aggravated I won't ejaculate in his ass
> – "Marshall Mathers"

No matter, critics love this record. "It's mean-spirited, profane, shocking—and actually quite entertaining if not taken too seriously," the *Arizona Republic* opined. "Guilty pleasures rarely get as good as this," added *CDNow* in a record review. "A bona fide masterpiece," raved VH1.com, adding that Eminem is "possibly the greatest storyteller in all of hip-hop."

The new record "may be among the most objectionable albums ever to receive mainstream release, but that does not make it a bad album," Alona Wartofsky assured us in the *Washington Post*. "The new album from Eminem is absolutely outrageous. And I mean that in the best possible sense," cheered Neil McCormick in London's *Daily Telegraph*.

> 'Cuz if I ever stuck it to any singer in showbiz
> It'd be Jennifer Lopez and Puffy you know this!
> I'm sorry Puff, but I don't give a fuck if this chick was my
>   own mother
> I still fuck her with no rubber and cum inside her and have
>   a son and a new brother at the same time
> – "I'm Back"

Time Out New York thought this incestuous, quasi-rape fantasy about Jennifer Lopez was "sidesplitting." The *Times of London* agreed it was "extremely funny." *CDNow* insisted, "The man is fearless." Why? Because he has the courage to insult, among others, pop stars Puff Daddy, Will Smith, Britney Spears and 'N Sync. Eminem also has things to say about quadriplegic Christopher Reeve. Talk about picking fights you can't possibly lose.

In a cover profile of Eminem for the *Los Angeles Times Sunday Calendar* magazine, the paper's longtime music critic, Robert Hilburn, came this close to comparing Eminem with Elvis Presley, a tenuous stretch that won the writer an insightful reply from a reader in Studio City, Calif.: "Let's see . . . self-described white trash who raps about mindless violence, misogyny, murder, child abuse—one who proclaims 'anything is possible as long as you don't back down' and then makes whatever lyrical changes are required to conform to retailers' guidelines of acceptability. Gentlemen, please."

A few days later, in his review of "Marshall Mathers," Hilburn, like so many before him, apologized for the rapper in advance: "Eminem is simply exercising his creative impulses—putting on disc all the forbidden thoughts and scandalous scenarios that accompany adolescence and just watching the fallout." In other words, Eminem's the John Rocker [pitcher who caused controversy for racist remarks made in 2000 while pitching for the Atlanta Braves] of hip-pop (calling the slurs like he sees 'em), and music journalists are his hometown apologists who can see no wrong in their star.

Elsewhere, *Newsweek* explained away the "Marshall Mathers" hate by noting with approval, "He picks on himself almost as much as he does the people on his enemies list. . . . By flipping his razor-sharp lyrics on himself, Eminem subverts the smirking superiority that plagues mainstream rap, a wily underdog move that lets him get away with more than he could otherwise." That's been a popular defense, most often invoked right after '99's occasionally jocular "Slim Shady" album. But the truth is that "Marshall Mathers" is far darker and more disturbed than most critics are willing to admit. Which explains why *Newsweek* didn't include any new subversive lyrics of Eminem picking on himself. They don't exist.

> Don't you get it bitch, no one can hear you?
> Now shut the fuck up and get what's comin' to you
> You were supposed to love me [sounds of Kim choking]
> NOW BLEED! BITCH BLEED!
> BLEED! BITCH BLEED! BLEED!
> – "Kim," a song about Eminem's wife

When you get done parsing the critics' language and logic about how it's all just satire, or cartoons, or Eminem's alter ego talking, the bottom line is that they've given Eminem a pass. Regardless of what he raps about, because he's so dynamic and funny on the mike (which he can be) and his beats are so tight (which they are), his lyrics are irrelevant. Makes you wonder what it would take for music journalists to sit up and take offense. A song or two about lynching bothersome blacks, or gassing a few Jews? Even then, it'd probably be a close call.

One thing is for sure, ever since the release of "The Slim Shady LP" in 1999, critics have been working overtime trying to soften his gruesome lyrics. In analogy after analogy reviewers have tried to convince readers (and perhaps themselves) that Eminem's odious tales are simply the latest in the grand tradition of shocking youthful rebellion as championed by the Rolling Stones (*Sacramento Bee*), [*Nightmare on Elm Street*'s] Freddy Krueger (*Times of London*), a Quentin Tarantino [*Pulp Fiction, Reservoir Dogs*] film (*Los Angeles Times*), the wood-chipper scene from [the Coen brothers'] *Fargo* (*Boston Herald*), shock jocks (*Washington Post*), [comedian] Rodney Dangerfield

(*Rolling Stone, Baltimore Sun*), the gallows humor of [rocker] Alice Cooper (*Los Angeles Times*), "the wink-and-nod allure of horror film violence" (*Detroit Free Press*), comedian Robert Schimmel (*Washington Post*), *Scream* and its sequels (*Times of London*), [comedians] Redd Foxx and Richard Pryor (MTV's Kurt Loder), "bombastic wrestling telecasts" (*Entertainment Weekly*), *South Park*, Jerry Springer, Howard Stern, *Cops* (*Sonic-Net*), a Robert Johnson blues classic (*Kansas City Star*) and the Beatles' "Run for Your Life" (*Kansas City Star*).

Really? Who does the following verse most remind you of—Richard Pryor, the Beatles, Robert Johnson or Alice Cooper?

> My little sister's birthday, she'll remember me
> For a gift I had ten of my boys take her virginity
> ("Mmm-mm-mmm!")
> And bitches know me as a horny-ass freak
> Their mother wasn't raped, I ate her pussy while she was
>   'sleep
> Pissy-drunk, throwin' up in the urinal
> ("You fuckin' homo!")
> That's what I said at my dad's funeral
> – "Amityville" (featuring rapper Bizarre)

MTV, which prides itself on running anti-violence public-service announcements, has embraced Eminem like no rap act in its history. The mighty music channel celebrated the new album's release with at least four separate Eminem specials. One was a biopic that gently painted Eminem as a wisecracking free spirit who beat the odds and did it all for his daughter. (No, really.) Another featured a sit-down with Loder, who asked Eminem about his gay-bashing, although not in a confrontational way. Instead Loder merely offered up an opportunity for Eminem to make nice. He declined. Instead, he told Loder that when he uses the word "faggot" it doesn't necessarily mean gay person, it means "sissy" and "asshole." Oh. "Do I really hate gay people or not? That's up for you to decide," said Eminem.

At least his producer and hip-hop guardian Dr. Dre was honest when Loder asked him about the gay-bashing on "The Marshall Mathers LP." Sneered Dre: "I don't really care about those kind of people."

In his *Los Angeles Times* review, Hilburn deducted half a star from his four-star "Marshall Mathers" review "because of the recurring homophobia." A nice gesture, although in the big picture it's rather comical. Why just half a star? And what about the woman hating that drips off the CD? (Eminem seems more interested in killing girls than fucking them.) Doesn't that constitute a deduction from the morals score card?

Entertainment Weekly tried to have it both ways as well. Declaring "Marshall Mathers" to be "the first great pop record of the 21st century," *EW*'s final grade for the album included a D plus for "moral responsibility" and an A minus for "overall artistry," which of course begs the question of what "artistry" is. And if that's not a clear indication that lyrical content is no longer relevant to music criticism, what is?

> Some bitch asked for my autograph
> I called her a whore, spit beer in her face and laughed
> I drop bombs like I was in Vietnam
> All bitches is ho's, even my stinkin'-ass mom
> – "Under the Influence"

A handful of critics have managed to break free of the Eminem groupthink—and they deserve credit. Christopher John Farley at *Time*, Renee Graham at the *Boston Globe*, Chris Vognar at the *Dallas Morning News* and Oliver Wang at *SonicNet* called Eminem on his horrendous, hateful lyrics. Yet none of them seemed willing to really pull the trigger and condemn the project outright.

Perhaps they remember what happened to Billboard editor Timothy White in 1999 when he wrote a scathing attack on "The Slim Shady LP," connecting the dots between the rapper's misogynistic rants and the rise of spousal abuse. "If you seek to play a leadership role in making money by exploiting the world's misery, the music industry remains an easy place to start," White wrote. The reaction? The music press looked at him as if he had three heads, with the deep thinkers at *New Times LA* so busy calling him names they forgot to actually read his column. ("Timothy White . . . publicly called for the CD to be banned," the paper wrote. He did no such thing.) Or look at what happened to Christina Aguilera when she questioned the playground bully:

Shit, Christina Aguilera better switch chairs with me
So I could sit next to Carson Daly and Fred Durst
And hear 'em argue over who she gave head to first
– "The Real Slim Shady"

Aguilera, portrayed as a blowup doll in the song's video, is one of today's platinum, girl-next-door teen pop singers, Daly is the host of MTV's hugely popular "Total Request Live" show and Durst is the lead singer of the metal band Limp Bizkit. All agreed the line about her giving them head was untrue. So what set the rapper off? Turns out that last year Aguilera hosted a special on MTV and introduced Eminem's breakout clip from '99, "My Name Is." After the video she told her on-camera friends she'd heard Eminem was married to his longtime girlfriend, Kim (which he was), even though Eminem rapped about murdering her on record (which he did). "Don't let your guy disrespect you," Aguilera urged her young viewers. And for that common-sense message she has been slandered in a Top 40 song that MTV can't stop playing.

Did anybody come to her aid? Hardly. In fact, the *Washington Post* cheered on Eminem's attack: "We're all tired of pop moppets like Spears and Aguilera, and he obliges us by slurring them both."

(And just in case you care, both Durst and Daly assured MTV News they were not offended by the fact that a new hit song suggested they were getting blow jobs from a famous teen pop singer. Oh, good.)

By defending and celebrating the likes of Eminem while willingly turning a blind eye to his catchy message of hate, music critics continue to cheapen their profession. They're also lowering the bar to such depths that artists will soon have to crawl to get under it. Don't think Eminem won't try.

Eminem's Gay Bashing Is Nothing New

Richard Kim

Along with charges of misogyny and promoting violence, Eminem's music has come under particularly heavy scrutiny from the gay community and its supporters for what they perceive as its dangerous intolerance. Richard Kim's article for *Nation* offers an analysis of this controversy from the perspective of an openly gay cultural observer who believes that the Eminem debate might yet be turned into a productive discussion about sexuality and tolerance in America.

DOES *THE MARSHALL MATHERS LP*—IN WHICH great white hip-hop hope Eminem fantasizes about killing his wife, raping his mother, forcing rival rappers to suck his dick and holding at knife-point faggots who keep "eggin' [him] on"—deserve Album-of-the-Year honors? This is the question before members of the National Academy of Recording Arts and Sciences (NARAS), who have, since nominating Eminem for four Grammy awards, received unsolicited advice from a bizarre constellation of celebrities, journalists and activists ranging from [Libertarian activist] Charles Murray to British pop singer (and Eminem collaborator) Dido.

Bob Herbert of the *New York Times* took the opportunity to deplore not just Eminem's lyrics but the entire genre of rap music for "infantile rhymes" and "gibberish." In a more nuanced report, *Teen* magazine asked, Eminem: angel or devil? and dis-

■

Excerpted from "Eminem—Bad Rap?" by Richard Kim, *Nation*, March 5, 2001. Copyright © 2001 by The Nation Company, LP. Reprinted with permission.

covered that 74 percent of teenage girls surveyed would date him if they could. The Ontario attorney general even attempted to bar Eminem from entering the country for violating the "hate propaganda" section of the Canadian Criminal Code.

But the most vociferous and persistent criticism of Eminem has come from an odd combination of activists: gay rights groups like the Gay and Lesbian Alliance Against Defamation (GLAAD) and family-values right-wingers like James Dobson's Focus on the Family. They all argue that Eminem's album threatens not only the objects of his violent lyrical outbursts but also, in GLAAD's words, the "artist's fan base of easily influenced adolescents who emulate Eminem's dress, mannerisms, words and beliefs."

In the face of all this attention to Eminem's "hate speech," even the usually taciturn NARAS is doing some public soul-searching. The academy's president, Michael Greene, said, "There's no question about the repugnancy of many of his songs. They're nauseating in terms of how we as a culture like to view human progress. But it's a remarkable recording, and the dialogue that it's already started is a good one."

As I have been forced to sit through all this Eminem-inspired hand-wringing over the physical and psychological well-being of faggots like myself, I've wondered just how good that dialogue really is. For one thing, so much of what has been said and written about Eminem has been political grand-standing. For example, Lynne Cheney, not usually known as a feminist, singled out Eminem as a "violent misogynist" at a Senate committee hearing on violence and entertainment. Eminem's lyrics, she argued, pose a danger to children, "the intelligent fish swimming in a deep ocean," where the media are "waves that penetrate through the water and through our children . . . again and again from this direction and that." Pretty sick stuff. Maybe it comes from listening to *Marshall Mathers*, but maybe it's the real Lynne Cheney, of lesbian pulp-fiction fame, finally standing up.

GLAAD, for its part, argues that Eminem encourages anti-gay violence, and it has used the controversy over Eminem's lyrics to fuel a campaign for hate-crimes legislation. While GLAAD and Cheney have different motives, both spout arguments that collapse the distance between speech and action—a strategy [feminist critic] Catharine MacKinnon pioneered in her war against pornography. Right-wingers like Cheney and antiporn feminists like MacKinnon have long maintained such an unholy alliance, but you would think gay activists would be more cautious about making such facile claims. After all, if a hip-hop album can be held responsible for anti-gay violence, what criminal activities might the gay-friendly children's book *Daddy's Roommate* inspire? Because the lines between critique and censorship, dissent and criminality, are so porous and unpredictable, attacking Eminem for promoting "antisocial" activity is a tricky game.

Thankfully, GLAAD stops short of advocating censorship; instead it asks the entertainment industry to exercise "responsibility." GLAAD launched its anti-Eminem crusade by protesting MTV's heavy promotion of *Marshall Mathers*, which included six Video Music Award nominations and a whole weekend of programming called "Em-TV." After meeting with GLAAD representatives in June, MTV's head of programming, Brian Graden, piously confessed, "I would be lying to you if I didn't say it was something we struggled with." Liberal guilt aside, MTV nonetheless crowned Eminem with Video of the Year honors and then, in an attempt to atone for its sins, ran almost a full day of programming devoted to hate crimes, starting with a mawkish after-school special on the murder of Matthew Shepard [a young gay man murdered in Wyoming in 1998], called *Anatomy of a Hate Crime*, and concluding with a seventeen-hour, commercial-free scrolling catalogue of the kind of horrific and yet somehow humdrum homophobic, misogynous and racist incidents that usually don't make it into the local news.

Perhaps understandably, Eminem's detractors still weren't satisfied, but given the fact that Eminem is one of the best-selling hip-hop artists of all time, what exactly did they expect from MTV and the Grammys but hypocrisy and faithless apology? And what do they really expect from Eminem—a recantation? Does anyone remember the homophobic statements that Sebastian Bach of Skid Row and Marky Mark made a decade ago? Point of fact: Marky Mark revamped his career by becoming that seminal gay icon, the Calvin Klein underwear model, and Bach, long blond locks still in place, recently starred in the Broadway musical *Jekyll and Hyde*. All of which just goes to show, if hunky (and profitable) enough, you can always bite the limp-wristed hand that feeds you.

Meanwhile, the dialogue among Eminem's fans has been equally confusing. Some, like gay diva Elton John . . . and hip-hop star Missy Elliot, praise Eminem's album as hard-hitting reportage from the white working-class front. They argue that his lyrics are not only excusable but laudable, because they reflect the artist's lived experiences. This is, as London *Guardian* columnist Joan Smith pointed out, a "specious defence." Should we excuse Eminem because he is, after all, sincere? Should we ignore his own genuinely violent acts—like pistol-whipping a man he allegedly caught kissing his wife? Others, like *Spin* magazine, have defended him as a brilliant provocateur. Far from being about realness, they argue, *Marshall Mathers* is parody, a horror show of self-loathing and other-loathing theater, a sick joke that Eminem's fans are in on. They point to how he peppers his rants with hyperbole, denials and reversals, calling into question not only the sincerity of his words but also their efficacy. For example, he raps about how he "hates fags" and then claims he's just kidding and that we should relax—he "likes gay men."

I don't know if Eminem really likes gay men, although I'd sure like to find out. What is clear from listening to *Marshall Mathers* is that he needs gay men. When asked by MTV's Kurt Loder about his use of the word "faggot," Eminem said, "The lowest degrading thing that you can say to a man when you're battling him is to call him a faggot and try to take away his manhood. Call him a sissy, call him a punk. 'Faggot' to me doesn't necessarily mean gay people. 'Faggot' to me just means taking away your manhood." Of course, using the word "faggot" has this effect only through its association with homosexuality and effeminacy, but there, really, you have it. Homosexuality is so crucial to Eminem's series of self-constructions (he mentions it in thirteen of eighteen tracks) that it's hard to imagine what he would rap about if he didn't have us faggots.

Eminem is, in his own words, "poor white trash." He comes from a broken home; he used to "get beat up, peed on, be on free lunch and change school every 3 months." So who does he diss in order to establish his cred [credibility] as a white, male rapper? The only people lower on the adolescent totem pole than he is—faggots. This strategy of securing masculinity by obsessively disavowing homosexuality is hardly Eminem's invention, nor is it unique to male working-class culture or hip-hop music. Indeed, Eminem's lyrics may be more banal than exceptional in the way they invoke homophobic violence.

Marshall Mathers reworks the classic Western literary trope of homosexuality, which manifests itself as at once hysterical homophobia and barely submerged homoeroticism. It reflects the kind of locker-room antics that his white, male, suburban audience is well acquainted with. So too were Matthew Shepard's killers, Aaron McKinney and Russell Henderson, and the perpetrators of the hate crimes MTV listed (who were, not so incidentally, almost all white men), and, for that matter, the Supreme Court, which recently held in the Boy Scouts' case [concerning the Boy Scouts' attempt to ban gays from its organization] that homophobic speech is so essential to boyhood that it's constitutionally protected. Herein may lie the real brilliance of Eminem as an artist and as a businessman. In a political culture dominated by vacuous claims to a fictive social unity—tolerance, compassionate conservatism, reconciliation—he recognizes that pain and negativity, of the white male variety in particular, still sell.

New Lyrics, Same Controversy: Why the Eminem Furor Is Nothing Special

Lorraine Ali

The most recent and virulent debate over the content of rap lyrics and the responsibility of rap artists has centered around rapper Eminem's music, but this is only the latest instance in a long-standing tradition, claims Lorraine Ali. Although particular artists and musical styles have come and gone and the content of lyrics become more sexually explicit and violent than before, Ali's article shows how controversy about the relationship between music and the integrity of American culture has remained essentially unchanged since the days of Elvis Presley.

ALL THE CONTROVERSY, CRITICISM AND PRAISE surrounding Eminem's 2000 release "The Marshall Mathers LP" finally caused a fiftyish co-worker of mine to go out and buy the album to see what all the commotion was about. It's not as if he was treading on totally foreign terrain—he did, after all, love N.W.A.'s "Straight Outta Compton" when it came out a dozen years ago, and has avid interest in most anything that rubs people the wrong way. He just needed to know what the newest source of outrage was all about. He locked himself in his office and came out an hour later. "Wow," he said. "This sure isn't for adults."

■

From "Same Old Song," by Lorraine Ali, *Newsweek*, October 9, 2000. Copyright © 2000 by Newsweek, Inc. Reprinted with permission.

He was right. And that's the point: pop music is an esthetic and consumer product targeted at kids between grade school and grad school, and often designed to irk their elders. It's been that way since young Frank Sinatra crooned to screaming girls in the 1940s, Little Richard camped and gyrated in the '50s, the Beatles championed free love in the '60s, the Sex Pistols spat on fans in the '70s and Public Enemy instilled fear of a black planet in 1990. Throughout each trend and era, parents have been deeply concerned and kids have done their best to keep them that way.

Things get ratcheted up a notch with every generation. You're not rebelling if you're listening to the same stuff your parents did; you're embarrassing yourself. Remember Jim Morrison's hammy Oedipal psychodrama in the Doors' "The End" (1967): "Father, I want to kill you! Mother, I want to . . . arrgh!" Eminem's cartoonish "Kill You" moves the ball forward by collapsing both parents into a single Bad Mommy to be raped and murdered. Those parental warning stickers may really be for parents, as if to say, "Hey, there's stuff in here your kid will understand and you won't."

There's a hitch. As every book about raising kids will tell you, children need limits—in part to protect them, and in part to give them boundaries to smash and trample. Generation after generation of iconoclasts, from Joyce and Picasso to Elvis and Marilyn [Monroe] to punks and gangstas, have gradually pushed the limits a little further. When N.W.A. dropped "F--k Tha Police" in 1988, it was a shocking moment. When DMX conveys essentially the same sentiments, who really notices? Even N.W.A.'s raps about killing rivals "like it ain't no thang" weren't so far from Johnny Cash's in "Folsom Prison Blues," where he sang of shooting a man in Reno "just to watch him die."

But in some ways, it is different. Johnny may have sung about doing hard time—and other things you wouldn't want your mama to know about—but his fantasy seems tame compared with the sex-and-violence- saturated lyrics that proliferate and dominate the Billboard charts today. It's a change that hasn't gone unnoticed. With hip-hop's current debate over whether rap has gone too far, insiders are once again trying to decipher what the dividing line is between true artistic value and provocative schlock. The answers will come in retrospect, but in order for the genre to continue growing, it's an important debate that needs to start now.

At the moment, the new frontier of rebellion seems to be against political correctness—the well-intentioned fear of offending any person or "group." In the 1960s and '70s, the fashionably rebellious attitude was to celebrate differences, to elevate the condition of women, minorities and gays ("Come on people now, smile on your brother"). That precursor to the P.C. ethos has now become the cultural mainstream; this election year [2000], Democrats with their many-colors-of-Benetton constituency and Republicans with their many-colors-of-Benetton convention are eagerly trying to top each other in their respect for each and every group that might be induced to vote for them. But in popular entertainment, and especially music, women are being debased in ever more degrading ways, excess and greed are extolled as worthy attributes and gay-bashing serves as a mark of deep-down daring. To be a counterculture rebel now, all you have to do is retool the vilest prejudices of your grandparents' day in the vilest language of your own. What's being promoted as the slaughter of sacred cows is McBigotry, with a state-of-the-art beat and no beef at all.

The result? Mainstream rap and hard rock, addicted to ever-escalating doses of defiance, can now feel as predictable as bad Hollywood action flicks. Part of the problem is that no really new style or scene has busted out of the gate since gangsta rap revolutionized hip-hop in the late '80s and grunge revitalized rock back in the early '90s. If there was anything out there in whatever today's equivalents might be of Compton, Calif., or Seattle, the entertainment corporations would have ferreted it out by now, exploited it and stamped it with their own trademarks. True, the Internet offers the promise of an under-the-radar musical bohemia where an alternative sound might lie low long enough to flourish—the trouble is, most stuff on the Web is so far under the radar that a potentially supportive fan base can't find it. So pop music has fallen back on the tried-and-true attention-getters—sex, violence, sex, consumerist excess and sex—and added the latest kinks in the Zeitgeist ["spirit of the age"]: misogyny and homophobia as expressions of free-floating countercultural rage and anxiety.

Another part of the problem is that we risk becoming jaded

and desensitized. When—as rappers and deliberately obnoxious bands like Limp Bizkit are proving every day—you can say absolutely anything you want, what's the point of saying anything? And how can you be outrageous enough to get anybody's attention when everybody is shouting at the same volume?

Of course, today's most vacuous pop—from bling-bling to Britney to Blink-182—will pass away, either because it collapses under the weight of its own decadence like disco of the '70s and the hair bands of the '80s, or because it withers from sheer neglect. This happens to the vacuous pop of most every generation: the musical equivalents of Chia Pets give way to the musical equivalents of Razor scooters. The kids to whom these fads are marketed outgrow them and are replaced by new ranks of kids, snickering at yesterday's amusements and suckered in by tomorrow's. The great hope of pop music has always been that in these ruthless revolutions and counterrevolutions a terrible beauty will be born. It was with Public Enemy, with Nirvana—and with Elvis, too. We can only hope we'll get lucky again.

Todd Boyd, *Am I Black Enough for You?: Popular Culture from the 'Hood and Beyond* (Bloomington: Indiana University Press, 1997).

Boyd argues that even though hip hop has allowed for the greatly increased visibility of African Americans in mainstream media, much of what sells still cashes in on damaging images of blacks, causing many entertainers to unconsciously perpetuate stereotypes. With a compelling mixture of academic analysis and pop culture savvy, Boyd casts his gaze on such figures as Spike Lee, Bill Cosby, basketball stars and gangsta rappers to examine the paradoxes and costs of contemporary African American celebrity.

Chuck D. with Yusuf Jah, *Fight the Power: Rap, Race, and Reality* (New York: Delacorte Press, 1997).

The always outspoken and provocative Chuck D., frontman for Public Enemy, offers a firsthand account of his experiences in hip hop, his often-controversial political views and activism, and his account of the social, racial, and artistic challenges that face African Americans today. Taking on Hollywood stereotypes, black-on-black violence, racism in the recording industry, and hip-hop culture itself (especially gangsta rap), Chuck D. emerges as one of rap's most articulate and incisive elder statesman.

Greg Dimitriadis, *Performing Identity/Performing Culture: Hip Hop as Text, Pedagogy, and Lived Practice* (New York: P. Lang, 2001).

Performing Identity is an innovative ethnographic examination of hip hop and its use as a defining feature of contemporary youth groups as well as individual identity formation. Dimitriadis draws on firsthand observations and social and musical history to craft a cultural study of the importance and impact of rap music and related hip-hop media on the everyday practices of young Americans. Perhaps most important is Dimitriadis' accounts of how young people's ideas of tradition, history, community, and nation can be constructed through hip hop mediation.

Michael Eric Dyson, *Between God and Gangsta Rap: Bearing Witness to Black Culture* (New York: Oxford University Press, 1996).

Michael Dyson, one of America's foremost academic interpreters of hip hop and contemporary black culture, argues that America's racial divisions (between older and younger black as well as between blacks and whites) can be brought into sharp focus by examining the social roles and cultural meanings of religion on the one hand and gangsta rap on the other. Dyson is especially interested in understanding how the disproportionate reaction against the immorality and irresponsibility of gangsta rap (on the part of both whites and older, financially successful blacks) allows for a noisy performance of public cultural debate that tends to avoid or conceal far more pressing issues of race and class—to the peril of all Americans.

Joseph D. Eure and James G. Spady, eds., *Nation Conscious Rap* (New York: PC International Press, 1991).

Eure and Spady have compiled a relatively early but still valuable anthology of firsthand material (oral narratives, written accounts, interviews, lyrics, etc.) that attests to the social and political commitments of socially engaged rappers from Chuck D. and KRS-One to A Tribe Called Quest's Q-Tip.

S.H. Fernando Jr., *The New Beats: Exploring the Music, Culture, and Attitudes of Hip-Hop* (New York: Anchor Books/Doubleday, 1994).

Through journalistic articles, critical assessments, interviews with some of hip hop's key figures, and social commentary, Fernando provides an often personalized history of rap and hip hop's musical and social evolution from the 1970s to the mid-1990s. A very useful introduction to the musical forms and technological innovations (Jamaican dancehall toasting, funk, DJ techniques, etc.) that made contemporary hip-hop styles possible.

Nelson George, *Hip Hop America* (New York: Viking, 1998).

Like S.H. Fernando's *The New Beats*, *Hip Hop America* is part musical history and part personal memoir of an engagement with rap music and hip hop culture dating back to its emergence in the 1970s. Nelson George, a veteran journalist and music writer, as well as a passionate fan of rap, provides an eyewitness account to the evolution of rap music from its earliest days to the close of the twentieth century. Along the way, George offers clear-eyed assessments of a broad spectrum of influential artists and situates their contributions to the overall culture of hip hop as it transforms from an underground movement to a global cultural force.

Bakari Kitwana, *The Hip Hop Generation: The Crisis in African American Culture* (New York: Basic Books, 2002).

Kitwana, a former editor of the influential African American music and culture magazine, the *Source*, proposes that we must understand blacks born between 1965 and 1984 as belonging to the "hip hop generation" (as opposed to "Generation X," a term he believes is useful only when speaking about white Americans). As the subtitle, "The Crisis in African American Culture" indicates, Kitwana argues that rap and hip hop, for all the exposure and financial success that they have brought to some African American entertainers, are largely responsible for keeping alive negative stereotypes of blacks without offering positive alternatives to counteract the disturbing social tends (increasing crime and murder rates, dissolution of family structures, etc.) that mark the post–Civil Rights generation.

Alan Light, ed., *The Vibe History of Hip Hop* (New York: Three Rivers Press, 1999).

Alan Light, one of the founding editors of *Vibe*, has compiled an invaluable anthology of writings from the magazine's archives. This multiauthor volume, gathering the work of some of the finest music writers in the field, documents the history of rap music and hip hop culture—ranging from film and television to fashion and art—through personal essays, historical overviews, artist profiles and interviews, and spotlights on some of the seminal recordings that made rap what it is today.

Denise L. McIver, ed., *Droppin' Science: Straight-Up Talk from Hip Hop's Greatest Voices* (New York: Three Rivers Press, 2002).

McIver's anthology gives a forum to a broad range of voices in and around the rap and hip hop communities, from music critics to African American scholars, to prominent rap artists who tell their own stories in their own words. By turns polemical, inspirational, informative, and inflammatory, this always provocative book helps a reader to gain a nuanced understanding of the many ways that rap and hip hop contribute to contemporary African American self-expression.

Tony Mitchell, ed., *Global Noise: Rap and Hip-Hop Outside the USA* (Middletown, CT: Wesleyan University Press, 2001).

Toward the end of the twentieth century and into the beginning of the twenty first, hip hop became a truly global culture. No longer is it simply the case that American rap has conquered the global market; now, nations around the world are producing hip-hop cultures of their own—"the expression of local identities globally through the vernaculars of rap and hip hop in foreign contexts." Tony Mitchell's collection of thirteen essays—a mix of musicological, ethnographic, and cultural studies perspectives—gives the reader a sense of what hip hop looks and sounds like outside of the United States and makes a strong argument that it will be up to rappers and musicians from Canada, Europe, Asia, Australia, and Polynesia to refresh the increasingly cliched rhymes and beats of the United States and take hip hop into the future.

Joan Morgan, *When Chickenheads Come Home to Roost: A Hip-Hop Feminist Breaks It Down* (New York: Simon and Schuster, 2000).

Joan Morgan gives a personal, poetic, and impassioned account of her life as an African American feminist trying to clear some space in the traditionally male-oriented world of hip hop. Morgan's series of essays touches on topics as timely and urgent as misogyny in rap music, single motherhood in the African American community, and what it takes to be a strong black woman and a "hip hop feminist" in the twenty-first century.

Alex Ogg with David Upshal, *The Hip Hop Years: A History of Rap* (New York: Fromm International, 2001).

How did rap transform itself from a critical voice on the margins of the mainstream to a global industry that now *is* a major tributary of the mainstream? Alex Ogg and David Upshal answer this fundamental question with a combination of music criticism, one-on-one interviews with key figures from the past and present of the hip hop scene, and meditations on the extraordinary adaptability of the music that is now the beat of global culture.

William Eric Perkins, *Droppin' Science: Critical Essays on Rap Music and Hip Hop Culture* (Philadelphia: Temple University Press, 1996).

Like Adam Sexton's *Rap on Rap* and Denise McIver's similarly-titled *Droppin' Science: Straight Up Talk from Hip Hop's Greatest Voices*, William Eric Perkins' *Droppin' Science* brings together perspectives from across the spectrum of writing on hip hop and rap music. This anthology moves from an introductory history of rap music to a series of articles that focus on virtually every significant element of the hip nation, from women and Latinos in rap to the politics and economics that gave shape to hip hop expressions to the cultural meanings of breakdancing and rap performance.

Russell A. Potter, *Spectacular Vernaculars: Hip-Hop and the Politics of Postmodernism* (Albany: State University of New York Press, 1995).

Through deft, critically sophisticated, and often kinetic close readings of a wide variety of rap lyrics, Potter crafts a persuasive argument as to why academics should take rap music seriously as a valid form of literary expression. Making the unusual claim that "hip-hop poetry was, possibly, the most important development in literature since Wordsworth and Coleridge in 1798," Potter pulls off a rare balancing act: he subjects hip hop writing to the analytical techniques of cultural studies and academic critical theory in a style that retains all of the energy, wit, and lyrical flow of his subject.

Ronin Ro, *Gangsta: Merchandizing the Rhymes of Violence* (New York: St. Martin's Press, 1996).

Ro's collection of articles is a dissection of the social history of gangsta rap and the costs of the cynical corporate exploitation and commercialization that has led to the merchandizing of gang violence as a form of mass entertainment. Ro's argument is that the music is no longer simply a reflection of street realities, but rather a direct contributor to a culture of violence, misogyny, and drug abuse that damages many African American and Hispanic urban communities.

Tricia Rose, *Black Noise: Rap Music and Black Culture in Contemporary America* (Middletown, CT: Wesleyan University Press, 1994).

Tricia Rose, one of the leading African American feminist scholars in America today, examines the many facets of contemporary black culture through the lens of rap music. Rose situates the musical and artistic expressions of hip hop not only in musical history but also, and perhaps most important, in terms of the social and political history of black and Hispanic urban communities during the period of rap's development in the 1970s and 80s. Of the many contributions and correctives that this book offers to hip hop scholarship, one of the most valuable is Rose's insistence on a critical reevaluation of the too often misunderstood—or categorically ignored—role of women in rap.

Adam Sexton, ed., *Rap on Rap: Straight-Up Talk on Hip-Hop Culture* (New York: Delta, 1995).

This is still one of the best all around sourcebooks for writing about hip hop by scholars, historians, sociologists, poets, and rap artists, as well as by some of rap's staunchest critics. An essential collection of personal essays and critical analyses that offers a kaleidoscopic view of the many ways that rap and hip hop can be thought, argued, and written about.

William Shaw, *Westside: Young Men and Hip Hop in L.A.* (New York: Simon and Schuster, 2000).

Part sociological field study, part survey of the contemporary hip hop scene in Los Angeles, the birthplace of gangsta rap, this book documents Shaw's exploration of the hardscrabble environment of the infamous Southcentral area. In his search for the truth behind gangsta mythologizing, Shaw offers a rare and intimate inside look at the lives of seven young men striving to make it as hip-hop artists and entrepreneurs, their eyes on the success and fame made possible by such heroes as Tupac Shakur and Snoop Dogg.

David Toop, *Rap Attack 3: African Rap to Global Hip Hop* (London: Serpent's Tail, 2000).

The third edition of Toop's classic (originally called *Rap Attack: From African Jive to New York Hip Hop*) is an excellent and well-rounded history of the development of rap music as witnessed by an author who has been documenting the movement and music since its early days.

S. Craig Watkins, *Representing: Hip Hop Culture and the Production of Black Cinema* (Chicago: University of Chicago Press, 1998).

A very interesting and specifically focused study of the emergence of a hip-hop influenced cinema, from the films of Spike Lee to what Watkins calls the "ghettocentric" films that came to dominate black filmmaking in the 1990s. Craig raises key questions of how films by black artists and representations of blacks in film generally serve to represent and misrepresent, explore and exploit the image of African Americans to both black and white audiences.

INDEX